OPINIONS
LITERARY AND OTHERWISE

OPINIONS
LITERARY AND OTHERWISE

BY

HENRY W. TAFT

Essay Index Reprint Series

BOOKS FOR LIBRARIES PRESS

FREEPORT, NEW YORK

First Published 1934
Reprinted 1968

LIBRARY OF CONGRESS CATALOG CARD NUMBER:

68-8499

PRINTED IN THE UNITED STATES OF AMERICA

PREFACE

THERE is an Italian saying that a Preface is the sauce of a book;—a device to give relish to the text which follows. But the subjects dealt with in this book are too diverse to lend themselves to prefatory comment. Indeed, in my leisure time I have merely put together under one cover thoughts which have occurred to me at times when an ordered expression of them was not possible. The writing of the book has given me a pleasant occupation during a sojourn in the mountains of West Virginia. The beauty of the scenery, the freshness of the air and the companionship of agreeable friends, have induced calm reflection and have quickened a spirit of good will toward mankind in general. If I have occasionally drifted into ironical or censorious expressions, they have not been actuated by any feeling of bitterness or intolerance or impatience. They have, on the contrary, been based on honest conviction, though sometimes unconsciously affected, perhaps even straitened, by attachment to standards and customs prevailing in earlier generations.

H. W. T.

New York City, September, 1934.

CONTENTS

CHAPTER I

GENEALOGY

THE interest in one's ancestors is not entirely vicarious. It is akin to the self-esteem which is the motive for many memoirs. In a laborious search among the records of our forbears we are sustained by the hope that we may discover an ancestor of distinction; and we take comfort in the thought that some of his qualities of greatness may have descended to us; or, if the dilution of blood through many generations makes a claim of transmission too tenuous, we may yet be inspired by a pardonable pride in mere kinship with the great man.

In the Western world there is none of the ancestor worship of some of the Oriental nations; and, perhaps, this explains why authentic records of the family history of Occidental races are not of such antiquity as those still extant in China and Japan, where the solidarity of races has been preserved from the confusing effect of bondage through conquest, or of infiltration of the blood of alien races.

Living Chinese families trace their lineage to Confucius, who lived in the Sixth Century before Christ; and in Japan the Imperial Dynasty is the oldest reigning family in the world, its earthly history having commenced in the year 660 before the Christian Era. Tradition attributes to the Dynasty an earlier Heavenly career. Even Japanese of noble families when, after the lapse of a thousand or two years, tangible records have disappeared in mists of antiquity, sometimes cherish a family tradition that at an earliest recorded date their founders descended from Heaven and began their mundane existence.

If the ethnographical development of the Oriental nations were a matter of authentic historical record, it would doubtless be found that the present Japanese and Chinese people are the result of the intermixture of races originally alien to each other. A similar process and a similar result have taken place among Western races, but at a much later period. The homogeneity of the Oriental people existed long before, for instance, the Angles, the Saxons, and the Normans had become amalgamated in what we now term the Anglo-Saxon race.

Pursuing the subject a step further, it is not strange that prior to the Norman Conquest in 1066 A.D., and long after the Oriental races, particularly the Japanese and the Chinese, had become homogeneous, people ultimately forming the Anglo-Saxon race were still engaged in internecine conflicts, and had not advanced to a condition of civilization in which the preservation of family records was regarded by them as important.

And so it results that among Western nations few authentic genealogical records, except those of royal families and of a few of the nobility whose valor and exploits have had historical importance, extend back for more than a thousand years; and even during that period tradition is the only support for much that finds its way into the records.

And what of histories of American families? Excepting those coming from the continent of Europe in the last century, such as the Irish, the Germans, the Italians, the Jews of Southeastern Europe, and the insignificant numbers of those from Oriental countries, the American people are fundamentally of Anglo-Saxon stock, tracing their family histories, if they have any, to England or Scotland. Leaving out of account the relatively few cavaliers who settled in Virginia and neighboring states, and who had generally fled from England for political reasons, the immigrants who became the chief influence in the formation of the character of the American people and contributed most to the creation of the great Republic of the West, were the Puritans and others who fled from political oppression and religious intolerance, including a sturdy and independent group of Dutchmen who settled chiefly in New York State and have been and now are conspicuous figures in its history.

But most of the immigrants I have referred to were of humble origin. They were farmers and artisans and traders. There were a few, and they were chiefly among their leaders, who were educated and of the professions; and they were chiefly of the ministry. Generally they were not of the class who took pride in tracing their ancestors by genealogical research; and their achievements in the mother country only occasionally were celebrated in history. In most cases, therefore, the family history of the founders of the American state covers a span of only three hundred years. And yet the pride of Americans in the early history of their Colonial ancestors has in the last half-century become so great that it has led to the formation of societies, (they are classified as patriotic), whose members can trace their ancestors in the Mayflower passenger list or as participants in Colonial or Revolutionary Wars or as signers of the Declaration of Independence. The antiquaries

4

of the Mayflower Society have by their industry
discovered the eligibility of the Taft family to its
membership, a previously undiscovered fact in our
traditions, and which, even now, I suspect is
apocryphal.

All of these circumstances have led to a keen
interest in genealogical research in this country, even
though it sometimes leads back to ancestry in Europe
which does not kindle family pride, being at best a
tiresome record of marriages diluting the blood of a
remote ancestor in the direct line, a numerous cata-
logue of children, and the humdrum of the life of
persons not distinguishable from the common mass.

But as family history interests many good Americans, it is worth while to consider some of the
motives and experiences of persons engaging in
genealogical research.

If a person chooses to investigate his forbears he
must be prepared to take them for better or for
worse; and the longer the line, the more the danger
increases that departures from rectitude may be discovered. Family pride may delete such unsavory
records, where impartial historical research would
demand that they be disclosed; and the more important the family the more striking the disclosure, for
man is prone to welcome the leveling effect of de-

traction, since that tends to make the whole world kin both in its strength and in its frailty. La Rochefoucauld observes that even friends are actuated by such a motive:

In the adversity of our best friends we often find something that is not exactly displeasing.

But what is the use of ignoring, or even belittling, the shortcomings of our ancestors that we find in our family record? If the record is merely for family perusal we may be to "faults a little blind"; but if it has historical interest, let us not forget Pope's lines:

"What can ennoble sots, or knaves or cowards?
Alas! not all the blood of all the Howards."

In the genealogical record of my own family, which I deal with in the next chapter, I find in multitudes of my kin-folk of the past no such odious persons as those envisaged by Pope. If they lack perfection, their faults are venial;—the ordinary type which has developed from the Puritan immigrant of 300 years ago. Others may attempt to trace currents of the blood of our ancestors which account for characteristics of the present generation. It is, however, sufficient for my purpose to state that my own immigrant ancestor came here from England about 1670, having left Scotland on account of conditions there, and was a farmer and a housewright (a good one, I trust); that he had five sons, all prolific enough to satisfy the Biblical injunction literally construed; that their father provided them with farms from his own holding, and that on some of these still live his descendants. I propose to deal later with a few things I have discovered in a voluminous genealogical record, even though they are not important except as oddities not uncommon in any genealogy going back 300 years.

Two things tend to revive and perpetuate the record of a family otherwise devoid of interest. These are, first, exceptional distinction in the public service, in war, in science, in literature, or in some other activity, giving to an individual of the family a reputation deserving of establishing or worthily continuing a historical record. From the standpoint of American ideals, distinction of a member of a family makes it a matter of general interest to inquire about his ancestors; and it may incite to greater effort if it appears that a great man has sprung from small beginnings. But an alliance with a foreign noble family may also become the occasion of starting a family history where none had before been thought worthy of preservation. Such alliances so often spring from sordid motives,—on one side financial gain and the other social ambition,—and so often and so naturally result in matrimonial shipwreck, that they are of some interest to show that too often their *raison d'être* is not what most Americans deem to hold out promise for a useful and happy married life. I say "most Americans," but I do not forget that the number of young people of American nationality who unfortunately enter into the marriage relation with too little thought of its nature and too ill-prepared to assume its responsibilities, is great. They do not accept the restrictions it imposes upon their freedom of conduct and they become willing participants in a joint adventure which ought to be carried on in a spirit of reciprocal concessions, if it is to endure. Too often the only recourse is divorce. This being a regrettable feature of our social life, we must avoid being too Pharisaical about marriages to secure titles, for it may be that, despite the ambition and sordidness in which they originated, they may on the average be as successful as those others I have mentioned which are too flippantly contracted. Perhaps the World War and its distressing *sequelæ* will discourage such alliances; for titles of nobility have greatly depreciated in value in the International matrimonial market.

8

But Americans with snobbish propensities do not discriminate;—the tuft-hunter cares little for character or condition so long as the gold-tassel brings a title. And recent episodes show the reaction on the titled person.

Thus an American quite free from any illusion of grandeur, conversing on the Riviera with a Russian Grand Duke deprived forever of everything except a meaningless title and a sense of humor, deplored the too obvious attentions of the American expatriated snobs. The Grand Duke with a smile said: "No, no, thank God for the snobs! What would we poor Grand Dukes do without them?"

The quest for titles came with the machine age and the accumulation of great fortunes in America. In the first quarter of the last century, the rapid accumulation of rulers of little principalities and their numerous progeny bearing the princely title, troubled some irreverent European writers. Heinrich Heine, the German poet, proposed that they be sent as appropriate wives for the American rulers. In his "Pictures of Travel" his satire takes the following grotesque form:

I imagine that we shall eventually be freed by America from this burden of princes (Note—speaking of the numerous German princes) for sooner or later the presidents

2

of those free states will be metamorphized into sovereigns and if they need legitimate princesses for wives they will be glad if we give them our blood royal dames, and if they take six we will throw in the seventh gratis, and by and by our princes may be busied with their daughters in turn; for which reason the mediatised princes have acted very shrewdly in retaining at least their right of birth and value their family trees as much as the Arabs value the pedigree of their horses, and, indeed, with the same object as they well knew that Germany has been in all ages the great princely stud from which all the reigning neighboring families have been supplied with mares and stallions.*

The fleeting and infirm character of mere titles is remarked upon by Cervantes when Don Quixote sagely observed to Sancho thus:

For thou must know, Sancho, that there are two kinds of lineages in the world. Some there are who derive their pedigree from princes and monarchs, whom time has gradually reduced until they have ended in a point like a pyramid. Others have had a low origin and have risen by degree until they have become great lords. So that the difference is that some have been what now they are not and others are now what they were not before.

* The translator of Heine's works, Charles Godfrey Leland (Hans Breitmann) makes the following note on this expression:

This prediction, that a time would come when Americans would devote themselves with zeal to intermarrying with any and every kind of European nobility or "anything with a title" is now being rapidly fulfilled.

CHAPTER II

THE GENEALOGY OF THE TAFT FAMILY
EPISODES AND ODDITIES

I RECENTLY came into possession of a voluminous genealogy of the Taft family compiled by an industrious but distant relative of mine. I have extracted from it a few isolated but interesting facts.

The original immigrant of the race produced five lusty sons,—all farmers. He was himself a man of sturdy character and became a very influential citizen in the Town of Mendon, Massachusetts, where he had a large farm which he ultimately divided among his five sons. He had no formal education. He could not even write his name. And yet he and his sons became a controlling influence in the farming community where some of them resided for over two centuries. The five sons had in the aggregate forty-five children, and so in the early part of the Eighteenth Century there was the foundation of a line of descendants that rivaled the families we read of in the Old Testament. One of the five sons,

Robert, himself had 12 children, 54 grandchildren, 128 great-grandchildren and 320 great-great-grandchildren, all born in the name of Taft. The females of the family are not included and might well bring the number of descendants up to 500. Of Robert's sons, Israel had nineteen children, his son Samuel had twenty-two and his son Gideon twenty-seven, the eldest born when he was twenty and the youngest when he was seventy-four years of age.

Perhaps in the day of which I speak the multiplication of the Taft race is not a very odd circumstance. Still, I have another motive in drawing attention to the fact, and that is to show that after two centuries of the blending of blood through eight or ten generations, its transmissible characteristics have been necessarily affected, perhaps even to the point of extinction. But habits and traits of character are handed down from generation to generation through force of tradition and these become less pronounced with the lapse of time. In his recent biography of his great ancestor, the Duke of Marlborough, Mr. Winston Churchill successfully disproved the principal charges of depravity made by Macaulay. But he was forced to admit the existence in the Great Duke of meannesses and the commission by him of acts highly discreditable, no trace of which is discoverable after the lapse of two centuries in his descendants, either through inheritance or by the influence of tradition.

In a country like England, where a noble house is of the ruling class, and where from generation to generation history records the life and achievements of its members, family traditions tend to survive and to influence character and action of descendants. In the ordinary family in America, however, which became a unit in the national life in the early Colonial period, the effect of inheritance and tradition upon the character of descendants becomes weak with successive generations, until with the lapse of time it becomes imperceptible. But sentiment may operate for a much longer period upon a too compliant imagination which discerns in a present generation the characteristics of some eminent ancestor of the distant past. I do not profess to be free from this human weakness, and I propose to "point with pride" to some names appearing in our genealogy, even though their possessors had not a drop of the immigrant-ancestor's blood.

Robert, the immigrant, was a Godly man. In his will dated March 4, 1720, he recited that he was "ancient," that he knew the "uncertainty of human life," that he called "to mind the mortality of my body" and that "it is appointed of all men once to die." After this somewhat repetitious prelude, he continued in a deeply reverent strain "principally and first of all" as follows:

> I give and recommend my soul into the hands of God, that gave it, and my body I recommend to the earth to be buried in decent Christian burial, at the direction of my Executrix, nothing doubting, but at the Resurrection I shall receive the same again by the mighty power of God.

He made his wife, Sarah, his sole executrix and his residuary legatee, but only in the event that she should "continue my widow, bearing my name," a condition which might seem to indicate an excess of caution, since Sarah, the wife, was, at the date of the will, over eighty years of age and a grandmother.

It is difficult to trace through two and a half centuries the religious experiences of the numerous race that sprung from the immigrant ancestor. But it was undoubtedly guided by the spirit of Puritanism, whether the spiritual yearnings were expressed through the communion of the Baptist, the Methodist, the Presbyterian, or the Congregational sect. Here and there appear rare instances of adherence to the Quaker, Roman Catholic and even the Mormon faith, but they are not so numerous as to have significance. The growth of liberalism in religious thought in Massachusetts and the adjacent states is more striking as a rebellion against the rigor and narrowness of the Puritanic tradition; and in the last three generations of my own family it took the form of adherence to the practices and faith of the Unitarian Church—a rather odd transition from one extreme to another, but caused by an intellectual reexamination of orthodox doctrine, particularly in Massachusetts; for it is something more than a witty skit which defines Unitarianism as: The Fatherhood of God, The Brotherhood of Man, The Neighborhood of Boston.

The development of liberalism in the later generations of my family was accompanied by a tolerance which accorded to everyone the right to seek peace of mind, and to satisfy spiritual aspiration through the forms, with the faith and even with the aid of dogmas, of any sect which appealed to their reason, their emotions, or to both. Through such tolerance my father was able to discharge without religious prejudice, his judicial function in rendering a dissenting opinion (afterwards unanimously sustained by the highest court in the state) in the famous case involving the power of the School Board in Cincinnati, on the complaint of the Catholics and Jews, to prohibit the reading of the Bible in the public schools of that city, on the ground that it constituted religious instruction offensive to their practices and convictions, and in violation of their rights as citizens and taxpayers.

In my boyhood days when my paternal grandparents lived in our home, there survived some vestiges of the old Puritan tradition, but it was steadily yielding to a greater liberalism which finally became firmly embedded, particularly as a guide and inspiration to right conduct in our earthly existence; and bigotry and cant were especially reprobated. In my impressionable boyhood years, I was not restricted in my occasional attendances at "experience" or "revival" meetings, at the Presbyterian Church, where a playmate several years my senior and not eminent for either a spiritual tendency or impeccable conduct, sought to bring me into the Presbyterian fold; at the Methodist Church where the vivid and emotional exhortation did not strike a responsive chord in a breast which had been taught to view even religious matters in a matter-of-fact way; or at the Baptist Church where I was more diverted by the immersion of the candidates for spiritual cleansing in the tank, which was disclosed when the trap-door on which the minister stood was lifted, than I was in the symbolism of the rite.

16

And my reason not having been convinced, or the influence of my home environment not having been affected, I drifted into the Sunday School of the Unitarian Church and occasionally (but no more often than I had to) listened to sermons; and if I learned anything more from them than to give a little more weight to rationalism than to emotionalism, I have forgotten it.

I have searched in vain in our genealogical records for an explanation of when and how my family forsook the dogmas and form of worship of the Puritans, and their spiritual descendants. There is plenty of evidence of independence of thought and action. But I have unearthed only a single instance of open revolt against ecclesiastical domination or of a refusal to conform to religious practice:

In the Fourth Generation after the original Robert, there came into the family, through marriage, one Lois Carlton, of Lyndeborough, New Hampshire. She was married to Caleb, a direct descendant of Robert through his son Joseph. She was evidently of a disputatious nature. In 1817, when she had had seven children and was about forty years of age, she incurred the displeasure of the minister of her church. This appears from the following record in the Barre (N. H.) Church, under date of August 6, 1817:

Whereas our sister Lois Taft has gone aside from her covenant vows in her unchristianlike conduct toward Mr. Timothy Bigelow in sending him the 21st chap of 1st Kings, and in her speeches and treatment toward him, has given the enemy occasion to speak reproachfully of the religion of Jesus, and I have endeavored to labor with her according to the spirit of the gospel, the first and second steps have been taken and no satisfaction obtained, I therefore feel it my duty to tell it to the church and request them to look into the matter and endeavor to labor with her in christian meekness to bring her back to her duty.

FRANCIS CLARK.

These are the accusations brought against me by Mr. Clark in the spring of 1817. Lois Taft.

First for telling Salisbury Bigelow to tell his father that I wanted he should read the 21 chap. of 1st Kings. For refusing to let Mr. Bigelow grind on the grindstone. For not lending Mr. Bigelow the hatchet. For not visiting more to Mr. Bigelows. For not asking Mr. Bigelow how his folks did when he came here. For calling Mr. Bigelow Ahab and his wife Jezebel. For letting Lois and Rhoda go down to his house fast day visiting. (very sacrilegous) For not being willing that people should come here visiting. For not attending meetings more. For going out of conference when he got up to speak.

Unfortunately, we have nothing further to show the result of Lois' rebellion; but it is fair to assume that from her militant attitude the Church concluded that it would be useless "to labor with her in christian meekness" and that to attempt to enforce any kind of discipline would make matters worse. It had to be contented with the reflection that the Lois of the Nineteenth Century was different from Lois, the grandmother of Timothy, for whom she was named, and in whom "dwelt first" the "unfeigned faith" of which the modern Lois was sadly destitute.

Probably the unrighteous Lois went on letting her children (then 15 and 16 years of age) go visiting whensoever and wheresoever she might list. And probably Mr. Bigelow had to furnish himself with his own grindstone and hatchet and to be content without a more cordial neighborliness on the part of Lois, and perhaps the visits of the two daughters were suspended either on fast days or at a less holy season. And, unless we misjudge the implacable spirit of Lois, she never withdrew the charge that Mr. Bigelow, like Ahab of old "did evil in the sight of the Lord above all that were before him . . ." and that he "went and served Baal and worshipped him," and that Mrs. Bigelow was capable of such cruelties as those imputed to Jezebel in the Holy Writ.

A hundred years earlier it might have gone hard with Lois. But in the Nineteenth Century evidence of a liberal revolt began to appear and church discipline was no longer so effective as of yore; and it was the spirit of rebellion exhibited by Lois that ultimately found expression in the liberalism of the Unitarian pulpits.

Undoubtedly the religious spirit of the Taft family was maintained through many generations, and among the thousands of the kinsfolk there seems to have been no heretical teaching or practice, unless the growing sect of the Unitarians might be classified by Trinitarians as unregenerate. But it is equally true that in the course of two and a half centuries and especially in the Nineteenth Century their yearning for spiritual comfort found sympathetic resting places in the faiths and rites and dogmas of other sects. Thus, Benjamin, the youngest son of Robert, the immigrant, early became a Quaker, and his children followed him into the company of the Friends. Without impugning his motives it may be noted that Quakers were not taxed for the support of the minister nor were they subject to military duty. In the early days the Friends considered inscriptions on gravestones as undue ostentation and they were not always careful to report marriages, births and deaths. As tax rolls, enlistment rolls and vital statistics are the chief sources for genealogical records, we know little about the descendants of Benjamin. But we do know that he "had a frugal mind" and when he died in 1768 he left a larger fortune than any of his more militant brothers.

Seth, born August 11th, 1798, being of the Sixth Generation, and Ezra Taft Benson, said to be the son of Chloe, who was born July 7, 1785, escaping from the family environment by settling in Illinois, further departed from the faith of their fathers by removing to Utah and becoming Mormons. Seth was one of the Pioneers of '47, the first party to enter Salt Lake Valley and afterwards held high office in the Church. Ezra was one of the Twelve Mormon Apostles who rank next to the President of the Church. In 1836 he had embraced the Mormon faith and was ordained Elder in 1840. He is said to have had five plural wives.

In the Fifth Generation there was a George Washington Taft, who died in Cincinnati in 1824. He was a devout Presbyterian. He pressed his children so hard to attend church that his son Samuel took an oath that when he grew up he would never enter a church, except for a funeral or a wedding, because his father required the family of twelve to attend service when the weather was so severe that they were the entire congregation. But despite this rigidity in requiring a semblance of worship the father had broad sympathies. Thus in a town where there was but one Catholic family and a nun was a matter of curiosity, he once hospitably entertained at his home two Catholic nuns when they were on their way to found a Catholic academy in Kentucky; and later he sent his two daughters, Julia and Caroline, to the academy when founded, as a result of which, and to the father's consternation, they not only became Catholics, but one of them became a Sister of Charity, and subsequently many others of their branch of the family embraced the same faith.

Inherited Puritan traditions were not always a restraint upon conduct, nor did they prevent evasions where financial liability threatened to thwart the designs of Cupid. Hanna, of the Fifth Generation, was born in 1758 and at the age of 18 years married one William Ward, who died insolvent ten years later, leaving her a widow at 28. She was appointed his administrator. Within a few months after his death she was moved to marry one Moses Joy. But by a curious rule of law prevailing among the early settlers of Windham County, Vermont, where the widow resided, a man marrying a widow who was the administrator of her husband and who through the marriage became possessed of property purchased by the first husband, made himself liable to

account for the goods and estate of his predecessor.*
In order to avoid this predicament, so that the widow
should be acquired free of encumbrances, she retired
into a closet, and threw aside all the garments which
would be an embarrassing financial link between the
two husbands. In a nude state she was invisible to
the minister and the groom, except for an arm and a
hand thrust through a diamond hole in the door.
The hand was eagerly grasped by the groom and the
ceremony was performed by "the jolliest parson in
Vermont." Having then been attired by her maid in
wedding garments previously furnished by the
groom, she stepped forth from her close quarters
radiant with happiness in the possession of a new
husband cunningly purged of the liabilities of his
predecessor.

The social austerity which we associate with, or
which is caused by, the restrictions of Puritanism,
showed signs of mellowing as liberalism crept in.
But still we do not look to Colonial New England
for the grace and charm and social instinct which,

---

* There seems at one time to have been a similar Scotch law.
A person intermeddling with the effects of a decedent without
express legal authority was subjected to a liability to pay all the
debts of the decedent. The rule was adopted to guard against
embezzlement, and its violation was technically called "vicious
intromission". (See Boswell's "Life of Johnson.")

despite early hardships, survived in the cavaliers of
Virginia and adjacent Southern states. And yet we
find in our genealogical history an instance of exotic
feminine charm flowering in the frigid social atmos-
phere of Eighteenth Century Massachusetts.

Samuel Taft, of the Fourth Generation, was born
in 1735. He owned and carried on a farm two miles
north of Uxbridge, Mass. on the old turnpike from
Boston to Hartford, and, as was the custom of the
day, he also maintained a tavern for the accom-
modation of travelers on the important thorough-
fare. The tavern sign was recently in existence and
bears a representation of the American Eagle and
thirteen stars and bars, with the name of S. Taft,
and the date, 1778.

I now give the narrative as it appears in the family
record:

> Soon after his first election to the Presidency, General
> Washington was travelling, en route from Boston to New
> York, by way of Hartford, Conn., and stopped for the
> night at Samuel's tavern. His travelling equipage is de-
> scribed as follows. First came a gentleman, in uniform,
> on a dapple-grey horse; second, two aids, in uniform, on
> dapple-grey horses; third, the travelling carriage in which
> sat General Washington, drawn by bay horses, with two
> negro boys as riders; and fourth, the baggage wagon,
> drawn by two horses. Samuel's daughters, Mercy and
> Parla, waited upon the distinguished guest, who was so

pleased with their attentions that when he reached Hartford, he wrote the following letter:

"Hartford, Nov. 8, 1789.
"To Mr. Taft, near Uxbridge, Mass.—

"Sir,—Being informed that you have given my name to one of your sons and called another after Mrs. Washington's family" (Dandridge) "and being moreover much pleased with the modest and innocent looks of your two daughters, Patty and Polly, I do for these reasons send each of these girls a piece of chintz; and to Patty, who bears the name of Mrs. Washington, and who waited more upon us than Polly did, I send five guineas, with which she may buy herself any little ornaments she may want, or she may dispose of them in any other manner more agreeable to herself. As I do not give these things with a view to have it talked of, or even to its being known, the less there is said about the matter the better you will please me; but, that I may be sure the chintz and money have got safe to hand, let Patty, who I dare say is equal to it, write me a line informing me thereof, directed 'to the President of the United States, at New York.' I wish you and your family well, and am your humble servant.

"GEORGE WASHINGTON."

From this letter, it would seem that Mercy was called "Patty" and Parla "Polly," but the General might have understood Mercy's name to have been Martha, of which the diminutive was "Patty," especially as Mercy's name was written by Frederic, her eldest brother, on a record, as "Marcy," the broad pronunciation of which might have caused the General to understand it as "Martha." Washington, who was childless, may have envied Samuel, with his numerous brood (of whom fourteen lived to maturity and had families) and that his brief stop at the Taft tavern made more than a passing impression upon his mind is evidenced by the following extract from the privately printed diary of the Rev. Amariah Frost, of Milford, Mass., relative to a call he made upon Washington, at Mount Vernon, in 1797, upon which occasion he was invited to dinner:—"He," (meaning Washington), "conversed also respecting his return by the way of Lexington, across the country, of the Difficulty of the Roads in Mendon and Uxbridge, enquired if I knew Mr. Taft's family where I put up that night, whether the old gentleman was alive, and added that he was much pleased with the conduct of his Daughters, particularly the eldest which he said appeared to have superior sense and knowledge for one educated in such a country village at a Tavern. She appeared to understand considerable of Geography, &c., that she was a very sensible and modest Person, enquired if she was married. I informed him she was. He hoped she was well married. I answered that I believed she was well married and that it was to a Person of Education who was a Clergyman."

This historic house is still (1910) in the hands of Samuel's descendants, being at present owned and occupied by Miss Sarah F. Taft.

Unless we attribute to General Washington an unusual susceptibility to feminine charms, it would seem that the sweetness, beauty and intelligence of Taft women of the Colonial period has not been adequately dealt with by the chronicler. But then, gravestones, probate records, vital statistics, tax lists,

26

and army rosters—the chief sources from which family histories are compiled—contain little concerning feminine beauty, grace and charm.

In the Fourth Generation through the second son of the immigrant, there was brought into the family line by marriage with Caleb in 1781, one Hannah, of whom a descendant writes that she "was a Scotch woman of grate strength. It is said she could take up a barrel of whiskey and drink out of the bung-hole,"—indicating not only strength but an irrepressible craving, which, according to the family history is singularly absent in the Taft race, despite their Caledonian origin;—perhaps it was their preference for "the cups that cheer but not inebriate" that was one of their motives for leaving Scotland.

In a community as small in number as that located in East and Southeast Massachusetts, where the Taft family lived in great numbers for several centuries, (a few only emigrating to Southern Vermont and some of the newly settled states of the Middle West), it is not strange that we find connections linking us with persons of note. The instances I mention are remote; and in neither character nor ability, nor in any other particular, have I been able to discover transmissible qualities having a similarity reflecting credit on our particular line; nor do they show inheritable vices which may be pointed to to explain and, perhaps, condone any weaknesses of our own. They are merely coincidences.

The immigrant Robert was one of three brothers who fled from Scotland. One of the brothers, Matthew, settled in Ireland and came to America in 1728. They were then known as the Irish Tafts. Eli, the third of the line, in 1790 married Esther Adams, a descendant of Henry Adams, from whom also descended President Adams.

Charles Edward, born in 1820, was of the Fourth Generation in the line of Matthew. He is the only member of the entire family who went to the South and became a slave-owner. One of his slaves, upon being freed, took the name of "Boston Taft," went to the West and as the chronicles say, this accounts "for several brunette Taft families in Kansas City and elsewhere."

Joseph, the son of the immigrant Robert, and our lineal ancestor, was born in 1680 and in 1708 he married Elizabeth Emerson. She was the great-granddaughter of Thomas Emerson, from whom in the Seventh Generation, Ralph Waldo Emerson was descended.

Another descendant of Joseph was Aaron, my own great-grandfather, born in 1743. He married

Rhoda, the great-great-granddaughter of Edward Rawson, Secretary of the Massachusetts Bay Colony from 1650 to 1686. During a part of that time, William Torrey, one of my mother's ancestors, was Clerk of the House of Deputies of Massachusetts. The Colonial laws of the period were signed by these two officials. About two hundred years later, in 1853, the families of the two were united by the marriage of my father and mother.

Phila Amelia, in the Sixth Generation from Robert, married N. R. Locke, the father of David R. Locke (Petroleum V. Nasby), who as the chronicler comments "thereby scored a narrow escape from being a Taft."

Elijah, in the Sixth Generation, was born in 1796. His wife had ancestors in common with Salmon P. Chase, Chief Justice of the United States.

Lucy Taft, of the Fourth Generation, through the eldest son of the immigrant, married the great-grandson of the famous Deacon Samuel Chapin, who founded Springfield, Mass., and whose person is supposed to be reproduced in the heroic statue of "The Puritan," one of the masterpieces of the sculptor Saint Gaudens.

In reading the record of the family I am impressed with the longevity of the descendants from all the sons of Robert, the immigrant. Robert himself lived to be 85 years of age, three of his sons died at eighty-four and the other two at 74 and 67; and sturdiness, simplicity, serenity and contentment stand forth in the annals of themselves and their numerous descendants. From this the mind naturally turns to consider how in the turmoil of the machine age, with its kaleidoscopic changes, its struggles for supremacy in material things, and the atrophy from disuse of our reflective faculties, we can grow old or, if we do, how we can descend from the peak of strenuous effort and be happy in our declining years when waning strength forces us to change our habits and activities long become inveterate.

Some reflections on this subject I reserve for a later chapter.

CHAPTER III

FORMAL AUTOBIOGRAPHIES AND INFORMAL EXPLOITATIONS

THE majority of autobiographies create a momentary flurry following the publisher's announcement. A review mildly favorable or severely critical may follow. And then they pass into oblivion, without mourners. The American public has recently been inundated by such publications. Interesting though many of them are, often they are merely the offspring of an exaggerated ego, manifested through the pen of highly paid "ghost writers." For such a "tribe of egotists . . . who are never mentioned in any works but their own," Addison had a "mortal aversion"; and the "tribe" still exists. After a brief flutter their memoirs are set aside among that vast number of books for which room cannot be spared on the shelves of a well-balanced library. And the reason is not far to seek. Perhaps the writer has nothing to tell except that he has amassed a fortune; while hundreds of thousands of his fellow citizens who could tell of their successful acquisitiveness, go to their graves "unhonored and unsung." If the subject of the memoir is "self-made," that is "played up." But what successful American is not self-made? The state has had a large share in the making of every man who has had even the rudiments of an education; and those who succeed after they get their start, do so by patience, persistence, fidelity and conduct inspiring their fellow men with respect, that is, by those elements of character which bring success, whatever the initial opportunities may have been. A long life based on such qualities is not spectacular, and success follows from the cumulative effect of faithful but routine service. This is not generally marked by episodes worthy of permanent record. Sometimes the type I have described is thrown to the surface by talent in self-advertisement. His prototype is P. T. Barnum, who started as a very good coachman and became perhaps the most widely known individual in the world. There are two kinds of such self-exploited persons,—those who seek to recommend their wares to a buying public, and those whose chief motive is vanity,—that vanity which "dies hard" and "in some obstinate cases it outlives the man."

In this day advertisement has grown to be both clever and Gargantuan. The modern advertiser sees little difference between showing the merits of his merchandise and (if it will help) quickening an interest in the details of his own life and personality; nor does he mar the picture by any undertone of reticence. Thus an International tea merchant who dauntlessly sought to "lift the cup" on the Atlantic, must have had difficulty in making book-entries of the enormous cost of his frequent but futile ventures; for it had to be allocated in uncertain proportions to sporting prestige, social distinction, inclusion in the Honor List of his government, and increased profits of his tea business. But he was never heard to say that his investment was unprofitable;— and he retained the good will of all, and in America there was little malignant criticism of his motives. Thus, our public is ever indulgent to persons who must introduce their wares to the public; and it will even tolerate fulsome self-praise, classifying it not as literature, or history, or as a study in human nature, but as a feature in a candid program of advertisement.

The growing necessity of such exploitation has led to a new kind of business—that of the Publicity Agent, or (to adopt a more high-sounding title, as undertakers are wont to exalt themselves into "Morticians") Public Relations Representative, who is sometimes in his activities not readily to be distinguished from the old-fashioned lobbyist. In every great corporation such an official is regarded as a necessity. There have been private banking firms whose advertising program and its adjustment of relations of governmental agencies have required the services of specialists; and sometimes individual members of such organizations have availed of such specialists to keep the public informed as to their own activities and have thus created a synthetic autobiography.

Among lawyers, as well as in other important professional groups, planned forms of advertisement have always been frowned on. Professional men must be content to enjoy the gratification resulting from achievement in court, or in the hospital, or in the library, or in the research laboratories; for on such things is their standing in their professions founded and their reputation with the general public justly appraised. A conscious, but furtive, effort, through subtle evasion of rules of professional ethics, while it often serves to deceive the lay public as to the merits and standing of a professional man among his fellows, ought rather to excite suspicion as to his character and attainments. In our great cities such efforts take several forms. Some men have free access to favoring newspapers and "butt in" with effusions on subjects not related to their professions and on which their silence would be more appropriate. As Dr. Johnson said, they make themselves *"publick* without making themselves *known."*

Recently, enterprising news-gatherers secure (by telephone) "flash" symposiums upon late decisions of the Supreme Court, or doubtful questions of law still undecided, or suddenly announced political happenings. Some members of my own profession consider that as citizens they have the inalienable right to express themselves on any question at any time, without any qualms as to their responsibility to the public. The frequent printing of their names keeps them before the public; and there are instances where with the newspaper fraternity, and finally with the uninformed public, they become transmuted into "leaders of the bar"; and their colleagues wonder why! But this form of exploitation involves a matter of taste; it is not inhibited by codes of professional ethics. Some newspapers print verbatim statements of certain lawyers on almost any subject, controversial or otherwise, without any discrimination as to the respect in which they are held by the bench and bar, and thus they sometimes become of the

> *"herd of such*
> *who think too little, and*
> *who talk too much."*

Self-exploiters do not always shrink at criticism or even abuse? Indeed they sometimes invite it. Contention, not peaceful progress, is the essence of publicity for them and news for the newspapers. Publicity-seekers are not sensitive; and detraction is a price some are willing to pay for notoriety, even though it proceed from judicial authority or sacradotal sanction;—for the unthinking majority will too readily believe that judges are fallible or worse, and dismiss censure by gentlemen of the cloth with the old adage, *"Nemo militans Deo implicetur secularibus negotiis"*—No one in God's service should be involved in secular business.

Three hundred years ago Cervantes put into the mouth of Don Quixote the following sapient observations:

You remind me, Sancho . . . of what happened to a famous poet of our own times, who wrote an abusive satire upon the ladies of the court; but not having expressly named a certain female of rank, so that it was doubtful whether she was included in it or not, she took occasion to reproach him for the omission and desired to know what he had seen in her that she was to be excluded; and commanded him at his peril to enlarge his satire and introduce her in the supplement. The poet acquiesced and did not spare her character; but the lady, in order to be famous was well content to be infamous. The same kind of omission was that of the shepherd who

36

set fire to the Temple of Diana, accounted one of the Seven Wonders of the World, only that his name might live in future ages; and though, in order to defeat his purpose it was commanded by a public edict that his name should never be mentioned, either in speech or writing, yet it is known to have been Erostratus.

How appropriately for Erostratus did the "punishment fit the crime"; and yet how difficult to defeat his immediate purpose! And how many examples there are in contemporaneous history of persons willing to escape from obscurity without heeding the effect upon their fair fame!

A sensational egotist may fatten on the momentary publicity caused by some act or word designed to produce that result; and the sensation will run its course before it can be seen whether the author is a sincere fanatic or a clever sensationalist;—for the moment, however, the public little cares which he is, but only that the result is interesting and plausible; for, if it is, does it not at least serve as good fiction?

There is a kind of sensationalist whose chief weapon is vituperation. He indulges in broad generalities. He may even incontinently attack reputation. In governmental affairs as a self-constituted and unofficial censor he too obviously seeks the "lime-light." His misstatements grow with the multiplication of his audience. He springs often from the professions which deprecate advertisement. The chief offenders are the politicians; but appeals to the public are a part of their technique and we are tolerant of their excesses; indeed, if they but knew it, they sometimes bore us. The lack of restraint exhibited by some bureaucratic defenders of the New Deal has saddened many who believe that, in a democracy embarking on our uncharted sea of governmental policy, exposition rather than vituperation is due to honest objectors. But my observations are directed particularly at an unworthy garb of sanctity which the sensationalist sometimes assumes, forgetting that he should be the apostle of justice, truth, mercy and charity, and that he is charged with no duty to arouse the passions of the public or to impose upon its ignorance.

Recently, a clergyman of the Roman Catholic Church assumed the rôle of castigator of iniquity in general. His self-assumed mission was as broad as that of Don Quixote, viz.: that of "redressing every species of grievance and exposing himself to dangers, which being surmounted, might secure to him eternal glory and renown." But the Knight of Doleful Figure sought his purposes, chimerical though they were, with kindliness to all and with the intensity which mental aberration engenders—and with no thought of personal aggrandizement. Cervantes created a lovable character. The priest referred to, however, sought to achieve results no less unattainable than those aimed at by the Knight, but his methods were marked by half-truths incident to a superficial knowledge and, unfortunately, he sometimes exhibited a spirit of malignity. A New York clergyman has recently referred to the "Radio" priest's "attractive sincerity" which was "now transformed into insufferable arrogance."

The Reverend Father has had an enormous radio audience and his potentiality for good or bad has been extensive. There are many who credit him with the courage of Luther, because by his flagrant sensationalism he was boldly risking disciplinary penalties that might be visited upon him by his superiors in the hierarchy. That the Church disapproved of his methods was probably true; for his intemperance has been incompatible with its usual procedure in basing its teaching and its action upon justice and right, without clothing its edicts in inflammatory and violent phrase.

But the Church exhibited a statesman-like sagacity in avoiding the danger of making a martyr of the priest. There was some truth intermingled with the reckless charges he made against individuals and classes, and any attempt to separate the true from the false would have been futile. To call upon him to justify his excursions into unsound teachings upon financial and economic matters, would merely have led to showing that he had accepted theories of others; and as for his diatribes, it could be assumed that their very vehemence and malignity would defeat their purpose. It would have been difficult satisfactorily to test the sincerity of the priest or to determine whether he is a modern Savonarola or a latter-day sensationalist trying to imitate Aretino.

I have thus pointed out a few examples of self-advertisers. We find them also among the clergy of all denominations. The publication of sermons probably does good; but it also offers to clergymen (particularly of the modern type), a temptation to deal with controversial secular matters, instead of exhorting and counseling and comforting members of their congregations. A public discussion of economic and political affairs, tends to lead enthusiastic and impressionable young preachers into sensational flights.

Nothing so justifies memoirs as episodes contributing sensibly to the advancement of knowledge, the benefit of the human race, the advancement of science and the arts, the spiritual and physical welfare of one's fellow countrymen, and the development and elevation of the standards of literature and the fine arts. But memoirs which merely record the humdrum life of a successful professional or business man who is endowed with elements of success and during his life has done for his own aggrandizement precisely what millions of his fellow citizens have been doing, soon cease to have value except as a family document. Their disclosure of self-appreciation, previously latent, may even detract from the esteem in which the writer is held.

Anything more than a record of actual achievement, well authenticated, is vulnerable on account of the bias of a biographer, and may distort his treatment of his subject. Froude, a great essayist and historian, but by no means free himself from prejudice, and frequently charged with inaccuracy, has something to say on this subject. His critics would not hesitate to apply it to himself. In his "Life and Letters of Erasmus," he says:

The princes, statesmen, thinkers, who have played a great part in the direction of human affairs, have been men of superior character, men in whose presence ordinary persons are conscious of inferiority. Their biographers— writers of history—are of a commoner metal. They resent, perhaps unconsciously, the sense that they stand on a lower level, and revenge their humiliation when they come to describe great men, by attributing to them the motives which influence themselves. Unable to conceive, or unwilling to admit, that men of lofty character may have had other objects than are familiar to their personal experience, they delight to show that the great were not great after all but were very poor creatures, inferior, when the truth is known about them and the relator of their actions; and they have thus reduced history to the dung-heap of humiliating nonsense, which a large part of it has unfortunately become.

But there can be no such tendency among writers of autobiography. It is human that we should wish to present ourselves to the public in a favorable light. Any over-drawing may be due to honest, if mistaken, conviction, to defective memory or to unconscious exaggeration. Where there is no corroborative documentary or epistolary evidence, a record of great accomplishments may be highly interesting; but they are not always convincing, for most men are prone to believe that action taken by themselves is potent in bringing about results for which they claim credit. Critics have found a striking instance presented in the "Intimate Papers of Colonel House," written after President Wilson's death. Many admirers of Mr. Wilson have been disinclined to accept the implications implicit in the book as to the apportionment between Mr. Wilson and Colonel House of the credit for major achievements in the

Peace Conference; and it remains to be seen how the statements in the book will survive modern scientific historical research.

Of some autobiographies we do not feel inclined to be critical because their episodes are realistic and exhibit personal characteristics which, while they may not be valuable as a basis for making an appraisal of the moral and intellectual qualities of the writer, bring us into intimate contact with the lives of those we have esteemed as distinguished and thus engage our attention. The autobiographies of Benjamin Franklin and Benvenuto Cellini and the "Confessions of Rousseau" are examples of this, but with much in addition that has substantial value. The *Apologia pro vita sua* of Cardinal Newman is a wonderful exposition of spiritual experience of one of the purest souls and finest of intellects in history. But it was written for a serious purpose. It was not by way of atonement or apology for wrong, but a vindication based on a consciousness of right. It is a masterpiece of English prose; but it makes no bid for popular applause through episodes of human interest so commonly forming a large part of the typical autobiography; nor can its noble and lofty arguments, defensive or exegetic, be imputed to insincerity or vanity or meanness or self-exaltation.

But despite its value as a human document and as a literary achievement, it does not present a model for autobiographies that would have contemporaneous popularity. Furthermore, it will probably stand forever without imitation. Such spiritual experiences are rare and still more uncommon is Cardinal Newman's power of literary expression.

Luther was militant and almost violent and his struggle against abuses in the Church exhibited less of spirituality than of contention. His unshrinking contest against the Church organization had much of the dramatic and human qualities, out of which interesting and notable autobiographies may be constructed. But less striking for that purpose was the life of Eramsus who was no less spiritual than Luther. He was no more tolerant than Luther of the abuses which moved the latter to rebel. But he was moved by what he believed to be a more profound philosophy from which he deduced that the Church could be reformed from within. He said:

Many great persons have entreated me to support Luther. I have answered always that I will support him when he is on the Catholic side. They have asked me to draw up a formula of faith. I replied that I know of none save the creed of the Catholic Church, and I advise everyone who consults me to submit to the Pope. I was the first to oppose the publication of Luther's books. I recommended Luther himself to publishing nothing revolutionary. I feared always that revolution would be the end, and I would have done more had I not been afraid that *I might be found fighting against the spirit of God.*

There is nothing spectacular about this attitude. Quiet sadness pervades it; and it was obviously sincere. But in spite of the gift of forceful literary expression and the profundity of his philosophical speculation, his life lacked the dramatic features of Luther; and there are those who point to the epoch in religious organization brought about by Luther, and cite the attitude of Erasmus in relation to that great movement, to the latter's disparagement.

But I turn from such men as Newman, Luther and Erasmus, whose fame and accomplishments were so great that they were certain to be adequately presented to the world through historical literature. With such men there was little need that they should themselves supply the kind of personal, anecdotal, gossipy, often apocryphal, and generally eulogistic, material, which predominates in autobiographies or memoirs of men whose careers do not so stand out from the mass of their fellows as to justify permanent record. But perhaps even such material may be molded into artistic form by a "ghost writer" and that medium of expression may give it a vogue for a day; but it must have unusual merit if it requires a second printing.

And yet the love of humanity for the personal, the intimate, the anecdotal, is such that it accounts for the preservation for nearly two thousand years of the biographies and sketches of Plutarch and Suetonius, frequently quoted as authentic history, but probably filled with inaccuracies and illustrative anecdotes of doubtful authenticity. Perhaps writers of modern autobiographies are sustained by the thought that, a thousand or two years hence, when their books are disinterred from a dust heap, their literary merit may resuscitate them, as "quaint and curious volumes of forgotten lore," and as authentic accounts of the lives of worthies of earlier centuries, overlooked by historians of the period.

But I would not confine my comments alone to autobiographies that ought not to be written. For there are many which have added to the sum of human knowledge, have built upon lessons taught by great men in history, and have entertained their readers. I mention one recently published, that of Prince von Bülow. His memoirs fill four huge volumes. That they are highly discursive would not be a serious defect, if the narrative was not so frequently suspended by the insertion of such things as tedious character sketches, episodes and genealogical records of persons who have little or no connection with the important events described, or the principal participants. From the standpoint of literary artistry the book would have been vastly improved if condensed into two, instead of four, volumes—and it would then have had more readers. I read the memoirs in the English translation (admirably done), as my recollection of the grammatical construction and etymology of the German language is somewhat faded after many years. But with even my limited knowledge I feel disposed to charge Prince von Bülow with some, at least, of the "seven deadly sins of excess" in the German language, viz.:

(1) too many volumes in the language; (2) too many sentences in a volume; (3) too many words in a sentence; (4) too many syllables in a word; (5) too many letters in a syllable; (6) too many strokes in a letter; (7) too much black in a stroke. (See Appendix by Prof. de Morgan to the Diary of Henry Crabb Robinson.)

Considered from the standpoint of Prince von Bülow's purpose of presenting himself in the most favorable light as one of Germany's greatest statesmen and enhancing the reputation which he had earned during his eight years as Chancellor of the Reich, the book is not a great success. Indeed, the

Prince may pass into history with a reputation tarnished by his revelation of a soul filled, not with gratitude that for eight years his Emperor had loaded him with honors, but with bitterness that he had not continued him in office indefinitely. Repeatedly he holds the Emperor up to ridicule and scorn, and then, as if to show an impartial and balanced judgment, he pharisaically adds that the Emperor had real talent as an orator or that he admired some of his other qualities. But the device tended only to show deep-seated prejudice. The labored argument to fix on the Emperor alone some of the more serious mistakes of his reign, as, for instance, the famous *Manchester Guardian* interview, is not convincing. When the Prince departs from the too obvious effort to exalt his own reputation, the memoirs are filled with descriptive, historical, political and personal material of intense interest and indubitable value; and it is expressed in form showing unusual literary taste and ability. But the entire book is not a model for such literature.

The autobiography of Benvenuto Cellini is a most fascinating document. It is that which saves it from extinction. It contains intrinsic evidence that some of the swashbuckling exploits of the author originated in the imaginative mind of the great artist, even if we consider the lawless times in which Cellini lived. But the autobiography has little historical value. As a thrilling story it will probably continue to hold its place.

In the "Confessions of Rousseau" we have an autobiography which is *sui generis*. It does not present a picture at all favorable to the author. It is interesting. It is the product of a powerful and original intellect, whose influence was a most potent factor in making French history. But in some parts of the memoirs there is something in the nature of an artifice in uselessly laying bare unworthy acts or traits of character in order to gain factitious credit for candor. It is, for instance, hard to conceive of an honorable purpose in letting the world know his despicable neglect of his illegitimate children. The "Confessions" make a notable contribution to literature; and they derive fame from the enormous influence of their author upon the destinies of the human race. But they leave us with a lessened respect and even a feeling of repugnance that any man should so expose his character, real or pretended.

The most engaging, simple and obviously sincere autobiography in modern literature, is that of Benjamin Franklin. It is a model of narrative style, enlivened by wit, convincing in its candor and replete with episodes of human interest; and it presents in the *ensemble* a picture of the character of Franklin, unmistakable in its likeness and obviously faithful in its delineation. The peccadillos of the particularly human individual are not suppressed, nor are they laboriously condoned or accentuated. But they are not, as in the case of Rousseau, "lugged in" for some ulterior purpose. They merely shade the picture as the artists say, in proportion to their real value. Altogether the Franklin autobiography is the most perfect of its kind—that is, of those that I have read. It is a loss to the world that it covered but a brief portion of Franklin's life. If it had been continued, with its inimitable self-revealing style preserved, what a repository it would have been of the natural sciences, statesmanship, homely philosophy, expressed in witty phrase, diplomacy, finance, economics and trade!

There are other kinds of memoirs which have not the form of well-ordered, evenly balanced literary composition. And yet they are sometimes of great interest and often reflect the character of the writer perfectly as far as they go, but in a form not completely modeled. Such are letters and diaries. Their fragmentary, disjointed character, embodying as it does the interesting and the dull, the important and the humdrum, the momentary mood and the reflective ratiocination, the displays of intellectual force and the inclusion of the inconsequential—all these things make it impossible for me to read volume after volume of such writings;—and they can hardly be called stylistic literature. There have been cases where diaries have been condensed and their essential contents compressed in consecutive and easily readable form. This has been done in the case of the twelve bulky volumes of John Quincy Adams and the hardly less voluminous diary or memoranda or reflections of Ralph Waldo Emerson. Despite the sweet picture of domestic and social life so fully and attractively portrayed in the ten volumes of "Madame de Sévigné's Letters," I wonder if anyone has ever read them through. Even "Lord Chesterfield's Letters" one reads with intermittent attention, often with wavering eyelids, and with recurrent curiosity to know what response the son made to the indulgent father. I have found Cicero's letters to Atticus and to his friends, and "Pliny's Letters," more engaging than letters of most modern correspondents. But in these latter days such letters as those of William James, are delightful and stimulating. Finally, I cannot omit to mention the Prince of diarists, Pepys "that odd, vain little gentleman who chattered his

way somehow into the circle of the immortals."
Even his amazing record must be taken in small
doses. But when it has been read and its contents
absorbed, there emerges (much as a cinema picture
finally appears through the confusion of lights as
the operator seems to feel for the exact focus),
a clear picture of every phase, good and bad, of the
character of the diarist. I know of no condensation
of the famous diary which satisfactorily eliminates
repetitions, trivialities (they sometimes may not be
omitted), and inconsequent passages, and arranges
the rest in a condensed form, with some heed to the
rules of good literary composition. Something of
this kind, with some historical additions, has been
recently attempted in Mr. Arthur Bryant's book,
"The Man in the Making," but it is too brief to do
justice to the subject.

No memoir in the form of letters shows a deeper
sincerity in the love of her husband and her deep
distress as to her treatment by her son, than is set
forth in the "Letters of Empress Frederick." The
Kaiser objected to their publication in Germany, but
I do not recall that he ever answered their condem-
natory statements.

As an illustration of a diary having historical
value which at the same time exhibits the character

and accomplishments of the author, the "Diary of Townsend Harris," recently published, accomplishes every purpose of a well-constructed and worth while autobiography. It presents in interesting detail how, after Commodore Perry had induced (or rather coerced) the Japanese government to abandon its policy of national isolation, Mr. Harris, after years of effort, succeeded in establishing friendly relations between Japan and this country. No less graphic and interesting is the "Diary of De Maisse," the Special Ambassador of the King of France to the Court of Queen Elizabeth. What he records throws a light upon the great Queen and her personal habits and appearance, which the ordinary process of historical research would not disclose, but which are valuable in making a synthetic estimate of Elizabeth's character.

I have thus selected a few memoirs, letters and diaries to illustrate some of the things which have made the publication of such compositions worth while. A word more as to other kinds of memoirs. In the life of a man (or of a woman) there have been episodes or adventures, unusual and interesting. To recount these is justifiable. But to convert them into a vehicle for "filling" concerning the genealogy and life of the author, who has nothing notable to record, is sometimes the result of a vanity stimulated by a publisher who wishes to produce a bulky volume. Stories of travels, discoveries, exploration, marked leadership in thought and philanthropy, achievements in war or peace, or scientific research, distinction in the public service—such things as these naturally arouse our interest in the personal and family history of authors of memoirs and justify their publication. But the fact that a merchant has outstripped his competitors in acquiring a little more money after years of close attention to the details of business; or a lawyer during a practice of many years has been classified by newspaper reporters as a "leader of the bar"; or in some other occupation a man has achieved success a little greater than his associates and has been honorable and highminded and charitable;—it is rarely that such men as these have qualities or experiences that make it suitable that they should be recorded in print. And when they are, it too frequently happens that a "ghost writer" is employed to give color to the colorless, to add zest to the prosaic and to give a finish in literary form, or sometimes in the journalistic jargon, euphemistically called "popular style." An awakened vanity does the rest! Sometimes this happens in journals of travel and adventure. Not many years ago a party penetrated unexplored and unsettled regions of another continent. One of the party, a trained journalist, published a putative account of the journey into the jungle, and in such an attractive form that it had for a brief season a wide sale. Another member of the expedition stated that a large part of the thrilling account was written on the steamer carrying them to the place where their exploration was to begin. Piqued by the inaccuracies and inadequacy of his journalistic companion's story, he himself is preparing a book for publication, every phrase of which is to be the work of a "ghost writer," to whom he daily recounts facts which are recorded in a style having no similarity to his own, if, indeed, he has what by any distortion could be termed a style. And yet if the result is an interesting, and, perhaps, a fairly well-written book, what cares the incurious reader, provided the story is engrossing; and why should he be concerned that a meddlesome person ungraciously seeks to disillusion him?

I remember many years ago reading with unusual interest a well-written book purporting to contain the diary of Li Hung Chang, the Chinese statesman. I later learned from an authentic source that the entire book, including the diary, was the work of a talented newspaper writer. I rather resented the interference of my informant and should have preferred to retain unimpaired the pleasurable impression I derived from reading the book. Another intensely interesting book—and informative as well— is "An Englishman in Paris," published many years ago. Its verisimilitude has been produced by a skillful writer; and yet it is a work of the imagination based on a wide knowledge of men and things of the period.

As recorded by Slatin Pasha, then in captivity in the Soudan, Madibbo Bey, Chief of the Rizignat said to him:

> Be obedient and patient; for he who lives long sees much.

And so it is. And if a man has experiences of more than ordinary interest and knows how to relate them, or even if he is willing and able to employ a "ghost writer," why should he not do so? And yet the "ghost writing" process is unattractive to me. It would lose its deceptive character if the facts were avowed in a foreword. But failing that, are not the supposed author and the publisher foisting on innocent readers forms of expression, emphasis, color and, generally speaking, literary style, which must convey a distorted picture of the putative author?

But perhaps I have been too dogmatic. If I had made a survey of the memoirs of men who fall under the ban of my classification it may be that I would have discovered that hidden behind the well-known facts of a man's life (disclosed by Who's Who or by Special Articles in newspapers or by prepared material for advertising purposes), there were qualities of character and intellect traceable to a long line of ancestors, theories concerning the philosophy of life and sound and valuable views of the decadence or the sublimation of modern civilization or the triumph of democracy. But unless such things form the obvious foundation of the writer's distinction, one must, in defense of his right to apportion his reading time, adopt some general test to decide which of the vast number of memoirs of all kinds and conditions of men are worth reading. By way of conciliating the publisher it may be said that one is frequently lured on by a review to purchase books, which after an examination of the index, and perhaps of a friendly foreword and a casual turning of the leaves, are relegated to a remote and inaccessible shelf, and there forgotten.

England is less flooded with useless memoirs than America. Adventures and episodes and achievements of British citizens in the far-flung dominions, colonies and possessions of the Empire, afford interesting material; and of that kind of literature there is much that is not only interesting and instructive, but also forms valuable material for more formal history. I recall especially Lord Cromer on Egypt, and Winston Churchill's "A Roving Commission," relating to his experiences in India and Africa during the Boer War.

Of the more reflective kind are the discursive papers and essays of Sir Ian Malcolm entitled "The Pursuits of Leisure." His comments on books and literature are thoughtful and urbane, and his style reminiscent. In a spirit of benign philosophy he deals with memoirs and autobiographies for which he has a genial tolerance. He says that he declines to be

browbeaten out of my favorite pastime . . . and I shall continue to read, or to glance at, all the autobiographies that I can lay my hands on,

despite the fact that

some of them . . . are written by men who have nothing to say—and say it. . . . Indeed, the necessary and conscious egotism of such books has its own fascination for me. . . . It is really not important, even if it were true, that most memoirs are written by people who have lost their memories, or who have done nothing worth remembering.

What magnanimity thus "to suffer fools gladly"; even at the cost of fleeting time! We have such gentle souls in this country, but they have less leisure. For instance, my friend, Professor William Lyon Phelps, long since advanced at the Court of Goodfellowship, has written copiously on literary subjects, and as his years have advanced, he has charmingly told us how "Happiness" may be bidden and has gone so far as to record his "Adventures and Confessions." If he would expand these and add a little flavor from "As I Like It," he could produce memoirs to which even a crusty amateur of letters would be forced to pay tribute.

I have already alluded to the importance, in most cases, of brevity. And that is especially true where the writer enters into long disquisitions and reflections portraying or perhaps inventing conceptions of his character of which no one has a suspicion. Of course, one of the purposes of a good autobiography is expressed in the words of Hamlet to Horatio:

"Report me and my cause aright to the unsatisfied."

But the processes of the mind of the diarist, if they have no reasonable support in concrete achievements, are "such stuff as dreams are made of." If he must embark upon a sea of self estimate, let him make it brief and discriminating; and in this I recommend as a model what Montaigne said upon his election as Mayor of Bordeaux, expressing his reluctance· to accept the office:

At my arrival I faithfully and conscientiously represented myself to them for such as I find myself to be,—a man without memory, without vigilance, without experience, and without vigor; but withal, without hatred, without ambition, without avarice, and without violence; that they might be informed of my qualities, and know what they were to expect from my service.

CHAPTER IV

BOOKS

IN the period of adolescence and young manhood, in school and in college, young men seeking acquaintance with English literature, read many of the standard works of authors of modern times, and, of course, such specimens of the masterpieces of the Greek and Roman authors as are prescribed by the curricula. What is generally the result? Is there cultivated a taste for good literature, or is there even formed a reading habit? In most cases the answer must be in the negative. In the case of the majority of graduates of colleges the books representing good modern literature are set aside in the struggle for position in the world of affairs, and reading is confined to light fiction, of which there is quantity production, and most of which scarcely survives a single sales season ôf the publisher. Perhaps after many years there may be a return to good literature and a re-reading of books—the friends of earlier years.

Conversation among men and women who have had educational advantages, naturally drifts to the subject of books; and one is often asked whether he has read some popular novel of the day. Generally I am forced to say I have not; and then I "counter" by saying to my inquisitor that I had just been re-reading "Robinson Crusoe" or some other classic. Had he ever read it? Why, of course. But then it is disclosed that in his boyhood days he knew the simple and engaging story as told in condensed form in editions for children's entertainment, but nothing, for instance, of Crusoe's revisiting the desert island after he had established a settlement, or after that of his thrilling adventures on the coast of India and China, described in the second volume of the unabridged edition. Nor had he any conception of the clear and limpid style displayed in De Foe's masterpiece, or the dramatic effects obtained by the purest of literary methods. A work of genius he had classified as a nursery tale not worthy to be re-read in mature years for a better appreciation of its human interest and literary merit.

The greatest of all romances of modern times is Don Quixote de la Mancha. It was the unaided product of the brain of an author, whose imagination created a character which, despite its aberrations, is the sweetest and most unselfish in the history of romantic literature (even including that of Colonel Newcome, Sir Roger de Coverley and Uncle Toby); and whose wit and common sense produced wise sayings and pungent epigrams, whose fidelity to truth no less than their quaint humor, have preserved their cogency undiminished through the centuries. The skill with which Cervantes has set the world laughing at the vagaries of the Knight of the Doleful Figure, and yet has left undiminished the respect for his character, is a marvel in the history of literature. And the drawing of Sancho Panza, "of the earth earthy," as a foil to the impractical Knight, is a triumph of artistic ingenuity. Finally, the book gave the death thrust to spurious chivalry, while holding up to admiration the fundamental and noble principles on which the order had been founded. The delicate satire with which abuses of the church are set forth and the occasional words of disapproval of war as a solution of human ills, undoubtedly had great influence when the Renaissance was turning the minds of men from senseless wars and religious oppression to culture and material progress.

Over the whole romance there is suffused a quaint and pleasing humor which engages the attention of the reader, even through the four bulky volumes of an unabridged edition. And Spanish friends have assured me that there are many references and episodes in the original Spanish, the drollery of which cannot be reproduced in English translation; to say nothing of the beauty of the literary style with which the entire romance is adorned. One of these friends—a Basque, a Carmelite monk, a man of wit and erudition, and withal a most interesting individual—was my guide, philosopher, and friend on a recent trip through Spain. He was quite as familiar with "Don Quixote" as with his Breviary. He revelled in the Cervantes' wit, humor and common sense, and the episodes which evoked those qualities. As we passed through each of the scenes of the Knight's meanderings, including those of La Mancha, he recalled what happened there and gave to the place perpetual fame. And when we reached Madrid, I saw in the windows of the book shop displayed in positions of equal prominence, the Bible and "Don Quixote"; and may it not be that with the anti-clerical republican government of Spain the public may demand the secular volume be made the preferred exhibit? Since my journey in Spain, I have re-read the famous tale in an unabridged edition published in 1817 in four volumes, and with increased enjoyment. And those who have regarded the Knight and Sancho Panza, his Squire, as merely grotesque and exaggerated caricatures appealing to them in their childhood days like fairy tales or any story designed to please immature minds, should re-read the immortal romance, taking not less time (for it should be read slowly) than has been occupied, for instance, in the perusal of the best seller of last year (1933), with its extreme length almost unprecedented in contemporaneous fiction.

But there are many other literary masterpieces of bygone days which richly deserve a re-reading, and particularly by educated men and women of mature years, to refresh their memories of books read in their youth. Many of these I have recently re-read, most of them with revived and intensified interest and a few with little relish. In the latter class, I regret to say, are some books of the highest repute in the world's literature.

Repeated perusals of "Tristram Shandy" do not stale its charm, nor dull its humor. "David Copperfield" retains its supremacy as a beautifully constructed novel and as a masterly picture of human instincts and passions. Its pathos has no tincture of artificiality and those who delight to weep will still find ample occasion in its pages. One may well wonder whether the fantastic imagination displayed in the "Pickwick Papers" as the setting for the play of humor, will continue during future centuries to make an undiminished appeal. But the lapse of a single century has not abated the fascination which Dickens' work has for readers of all ages; and persons of intellectual culture continue to re-read the book each year; and that can be said of few prose masterpieces in the English language.

Of quite a different kind from the works of Dickens are "Vanity Fair" and "The Newcomes" of Thackeray. The satire upon manners of the day will lose force with changes in social life and in the *mores* of nations. The wickedness of Becky Sharp is not new in the history of the world, nor is it, in other settings, uncommon in fiction and the drama. But an original conception in "The Newcomes" is the nobility and sweetness of Colonel Newcome. The drawing of his character has a permanent value in literature. How long through the ages it will survive it would be difficult to predict. For my present purposes it is sufficient to say that at present both "Vanity Fair" and "The Newcomes" may be re-read after a lapse of half a century with unabated interest.

"Peregrine Pickle" and "Roderick Random" are

both splendid tales, but Smollett's diffuse style (correct and stately though it is), requires more patience if it is to be appreciated, than most readers of today can or are willing to expend. Of the same period and with some of the same characteristics both in plot and style, are Fielding's "Joseph Andrews," "Tom Jones" and "Humphrey Clinker." There is a special reason for renewing an acquaintance with the novels of Fielding, Smollett and Richardson (a few only need be read), for they are the precursors of the modern novel.

What books may be re-read with interest is largely a matter of education and taste, and there is a vast majority of people who prefer to occupy their available time in current publications; and some of these, though without literary distinction, deal in a competent and engaging manner with worth while subjects, such as biography, travels, science or history. This field is very wide and varied and the choice is largely a matter of taste, time and temperament. There would be no cause for discouragement in this if it were not for the fact that the yearly output of works of fiction greatly preponderates over that of all other publications mentioned and that most of it has so little merit that it does not survive beyond a single year. So far as such fiction is read by very busy people for relaxation, it serves a useful purpose; but there is much fiction having proved literary value which would serve as well the same purpose. Two examples will suffice. Mystery and detective stories have great popularity. No more engaging story of that kind has ever been written than the "Moonstone," by Wilkie Collins; and with some of the same features, "Put Yourself in His Place," by Charles Reade, is equally interesting and deals with labor problems of a hundred years ago; while "The Cloister and The Hearth" ranks as one of the masterpieces of fiction and is a deeply interesting and erudite tale of the time of Erasmus. These novels are literature of distinction and promise to survive for many generations; and yet an inquiry among one's friends who have had the conventional education of the day, will often disclose that they have never read either of the books mentioned or, perhaps, any of the many others written by Collins and Reade. But similar comments may be made as to the works of other authors—for instance, Scott, Dickens, Thackeray, Trollope, George Eliot, Kingsley, Lever and Lover and Mark Twain, and in translation, Victor Hugo, Dumas and Tolstoi—to mention but a few.

I have recently re-read Victor Hugo's "Ninety-

Three," and Bulwer-Lytton's "The Last of the Barons," and Scott's "Ivanhoe." I do not know to what extent the reading of the modern novel with its quantity production is displacing the older order of fiction represented in the three books I have mentioned. But quite apart from their just pretension to be regarded as good literature—"famed" books in Emerson's rating—they satisfy the taste of those who yearn for romance, adventure and thrills, and reach a high standard of skill in the construction of convincing plots. In addition, their readers must absorb, without tiresome study, a mass of interesting information concerning the history and customs of the times. Such books as these should hold their own against the vast majority of modern fiction in every essential element of that form of literature—excepting in eroticism, as to which quality I quote from a better critic than myself, Prof. Irving Babbitt, who in his "Literature and the American College—Essays in Defence of the Humanities," has this to say:

Decadent novels and other fungous growths of a similar nature are not peculiar to French, but are multiplying with alarming rapidity in all the great European literatures. Modern literature has been more or less sentimental since Petrarch, and a morbidly subjective strain has existed in it since Rousseau, while of late a quality is beginning to appear which we cannot better describe than as neurotic.

In starting a library Emerson advised that only "famed" books should be purchased, and none less than a year old. And Schopenhauer warned against seeking books merely because they are new or are talked about. But, on the other hand, Tacitus, in speaking of oratory, said:

> Where change occurs we are not immediately to conclude that it is a change for the worse; you must put the blame for it on the carping spirit of mankind that whereas what is old is always held in high esteem, anything modern gets the cold shoulder.

The advice of Emerson was not confined to fiction; but it is quite certain that a large proportion of current modern fiction (shall I say ninety-five per cent?), would have no place a year after publication in a library of "famed" books worthy of preservation; and in a well-balanced library of five thousand volumes, it is probable that room could not be found for more than one per cent of such publications.

What has been said, however, must be qualified by saying that books of little or no permanent value may sometimes serve to give diversion or relaxation in idle moments, even though they be straightway consigned to the flames or the wastepaper basket. I have, for instance, myself spent some hours of my leisure in reading some of the tales of Sabatini; but I have preserved them as above the average of merit of the Dumas type of novel; but even they are pushed back into dark corners of a bookcase whence they can be rescued only after a long search. Sometimes such books meet an even sadder fate. An acquaintance of mine leased for a term of years a country house in which there was a huge shelved recess designed for books. Not wishing to supply books from his city home, he purchased at a second-hand shop miscellaneous books sufficient to occupy the shelves—and paid a price measured by the longitudinal foot of space to be filled. But most of the shelves were so high and the rest so hidden by furniture that the titles of the books were not discernible—nor the books themselves accessible.

Many people (a minority, however), have little time to read modern fiction—not that they have no leisure for reading, but that there are so many "famed" books that they failed to read in early years, and so many that they want to re-read that are as interesting and more stimulating than the mass of modern fiction, that they select for their moments of leisure the interesting books of substantial merit.

But some modern fiction has real power. I happened to meet Miss Phyllis Bentley, the English novelist, and expressed regret that I had read none of her books. I added, with exaggeration sometimes permissible in conversation, that I read no fiction except that written more than fifty years ago. Subsequently, she sent me her book "Inheritance," with an inscription that she hoped it would "lure" me into reading modern fiction. I read the book with great interest. It has episodes which are sad—even tragic —and its tone is sombre. But it presents so objectively the problems of life in an industrial region of England, where the author lives, that it convinces one that its plot and episodes were drawn from life. It is reminiscent of Charles Reade's "Put Yourself in His Place," since it deals with labor troubles. It is a work of power. Another modern novel of interest and strength is the "Good Earth," especially as it presents an authoritative picture of social and family life in China. It is worth reading.

Among many educated people there is a lack of interest in the Greek and Roman classics. This is to be regretted. While they need not take up the laborious process of translation (the recent movement against the study of the classics in school and college would make this increasingly difficult), or make an extensive study of the great mass of literature that has survived, a little browsing among the classics would open up much of present interest. Perhaps it would be futile to lure the general reader of today to study or even read the "Republic," "Lysis," "Symposium" and "Charmides" of Plato, or the monumental works of Aristotle on Philosophy or Natural History. Persons interested in those subjects will, without urging, read such works; and if they are engaged in the study of oratory, they will read the exhaustive treatise of Quintillian, and the later one of St. Augustine, on Rhetoric. But I speak of many writings comparable to those of modern times and which in style have some resemblance to *belles-lettres* of today, and from which it will be disclosed how modern they are in thought, and even in subjects, purpose, arrangement and form of expression. The letters of Cicero to Atticus and his letters to his other friends, are the letters of an able and cultured Roman gentleman deeply interested in public affairs and intensely human in his strength and his weaknesses. The letters have the quality not common in that kind of writing, in that the interest does not flag from the beginning to the end. And they furnish most interesting sidelights on events in Roman political history, more concrete and intimate than is possible in formal contemporaneous history. His short philosophical treatises, such as those on *De Senectute, De Amicitia* and *De Officiis,* as well as many others, are masterly in form, substance and comprehensiveness; while in good English translation they are readable and interesting. "Pliny's Letters" are replete with observations and information of interest to modern readers, while "Plutarch's Lives" still stand in the first rank of the biographical art.

The force, often descending into coarseness, the penetration, merciless in its pertinacity, and the earnestness, of Juvenal in his "Essays," make his satires among the most powerful ever written, in castigating and ridiculing the vices and weaknesses of his time. They have the strength and are somewhat similar in directness of attack to the letters of Junius, though dealing more with social than with political matters. The essays are not long and are written in a very simple and readable style. Among the later Greeks, Lucian was the greatest of satirists and wits. He hesitated at nothing. He even ridiculed the absurdities of Greek mythology and laughed at its most sacred deities. The plays of Aristophanes, sometimes verging on the obscene, are directed at current abuses and are replete with witty satire; and no modern dramatist who aspires to eminence in his profession, can be considered well equipped who has not studied his plays. Even in this age some have been put upon the stage.

Many other Greek and Roman classics may be read today by the general reader, even though he seeks not improvement, but only diversion; and he might alternate by reading one of the fugitive novels of the day and then spending a half-hour in reading Lucian's essay on the "Dead Come to Life" or "A Professor of Public Speaking," or the Tenth Satire of Juvenal on the "Vanity of Human Wishes"; or "The Frogs of Aristophanes"; or a few of the short odes of Horace; or The Younger Pliny's letter describing the destruction of Pompeii and Herculaneum by the eruption of Vesuvius.

As a counterpoise to compensate for the waste of time and still more serious results of reading too much light fiction, the public taste for autobiography, biography, history and exploration, has been stimulated during the last thirty years. Some of such works I have already mentioned. Others are Ludwig's "Life of Napoleon" and "Life of Goethe"; "John Quincy Adams' Diary," compiled by Nevins; "The Story of San Michele," by Axel Munthe; "Diary of Townsend Harris"; "Life of C. W. Elliott," by Henry James, and "Letters of Wm. James." I commend especially the "Roving Commission" (already mentioned) by Winston Churchill, a well-written, thrilling tale of the author's adventurous life.*

Of history, Professor Trevelyan's three volumes entitled "England Under Queen Anne," with the subtitles Ramillies, Blenheim, The Peace and The Protestant Succession, are a valuable addition to English history of a period not well covered before and are of permanent value.

I have spoken of (indeed, have urged) the rereading of books of standard value. But I find myself confronted by the proverb, "The counsel you would have another keep, first keep yourself." And

* Note. Others worth reading are Viscount Haldane's autobiography; the "Life of Tiberius Cæsar," by G. F. Baker; "Elizabeth and Essex," by Strachey; "Henry The VIII," by Francis Hackett; "Alcibiades," by Benson; "Men of Art", by Craven; "Life of Swift," by Van Doren; "Life of Wellington," by Guedella; and of earlier publication, "Life and Letters of Erasmus," "Essay on Lucian" and the "Book of Job," all by Froude; the "Life of Machiavelli," by Villari; Lord Acton's "Letters to Mary Gladstone"; "Letters" of W. H. Hudson; De Maisse—"A Journal of an Ambassador to Elizabeth from Henry the Fourth of France"; "Oliver's Secretary—Milton," by Raymond; "Life of Roosevelt," by Pringle; "Life of Cleveland," by Nevins; "Aristophanes—A Study," by Gilbert Murray; "Marlborough," by Churchill; "Samuel Pepys," by Bryant; "Napoleon," by Bainville; "The Edwardian Era," by Maurois; "What Me Befell," by Jusserand; "Life of Emerson," by Van Wyck Brooks; "The Man of the Renaissance," by Roeder. These are some of those I have had time to read, but there are many others favorably reviewed.

I am forced to admit that a single reading of some of the most notable books suffices. Curiosity, a sense of duty and a desire to have some acquaintance with a style of distinction, lead to one reading; but the initial motive often then becomes inactive or even indifferent. At the risk of seeming to be lacking in literary taste or in appreciation of the creation of great intellects, I note some of the "famed" books I am not inspired to read a second time.

Despite the limpid and simple style of Bunyan in "Pilgrim's Progress," and the deep sincerity, the moral detachment of the author, and the originality of the form and setting of the picture, I found the personification of abstract moral principles, the allegory and the labored figures of speech, so monotonous on a recent attempted reading, that they retained my interest only through half the story. However the book inspired the author's deeply religious contemporaries, it is difficult to see how in this practical and work-a-day age it could be effective to influence action or inspire faith. But historically and for its style, the purity and elevation of the motive which inspired it, and its once great influence, it is one of the great books of the world. It is too much to say, however, as one writer has, that the tale of Christian's struggles and triumph, still appeals to young and old.

Anatole France's "Life of Joan of Arc" portrays a character no less spiritual or heroic than that of Bunyan. But I found the author's style (perhaps because in translation) diffuse and tedious; and if I should wish to renew my acquaintance with the Maid of Orléans, I should choose a biography less ambitious and more interesting—perhaps Mark Twain's putative creation.

As an artist in poetic prose there are few equals of Walter Pater. But in "Marius the Epicurean" and "The Renaissance," the painting is often so idyllic and the thought so mystical that a reader inclining to the concrete in thought, directness of expression and freedom from nebulosity, tires in the effort to follow the writer's flights; and I was not inclined to repeat the effort.

The reactions from the reading after many years of the epic poems of Homer are worth a brief comment. The majestic style, the poetic creations and the heroic exploits lose much force with youthful students, forced as they are to concentrate on idiom, syntax, etymology and scanning; and they have little zest in later years to include in their general reading great masterpieces with which they never cease to associate their anxiety in their student days lest they should fail to receive the pass mark. And there is another thing which detracts from interest in the "Iliad" and the "Odyssey." They picture a theogony based on motives and actions which are at war with the principles of Christian tenets and philosophy, the conduct of pagan divinities being sometimes inspired by motives of selfishness, cruelty, jealousy, ambition and lust. There is bravery, nobility and generosity in some of the great human actors in the epic drama, but that does not rescue it from the charge that the example set by the Gods themselves cannot have an ennobling or even an elevating influence upon those who inhabit the earth. An interesting writer * has expressed something of this idea as follows:

Modern readers often fail to find sublimity in Homer where ancient critics rejoice in it. . . . Homer's imagination was hopelessly cramped by the narrow horizon which mythological traditions offered it. The battle of the Gods and the shaking of Jove's ambrosial locks, the leaping of Neptune's chariot over the sea, the descent into Hades in the Odyssey, and other well known passages, fall short of sublimity in our minds. In every case there are elements or circumstances of the description which keep it near the earth. The poet's imagination is clogged in its flight by the weight of the earth. His Gods may be bigger than men; they are not other than men.

And the author contrasts the productions of the

* "The Art of Interesting," by Francis P. Donnelly, S.J.

Hebrew imagination as being far superior to those of the ancient Greeks and elaborates upon that theme.

"Gargantua and Pantagruel" of Rabelais is a really wonderful satirical work. For instance, nothing in literature excels in ironic wit the trial of Bridlegoose on the charge of deciding the cases brought before him by a throw of the dice. But the gems of denunciation in the amusing cloak of satire or ridicule, all directed against vices of the age, and particularly of the church, are set against a murky, repellent, obscure, and repetitious background; and an abundance of filth and obscenity is gratuitously inserted in riotous and illogical order; and these things grievously mar the work. Except for the student or the critic or the teacher, it will suffice for most readers to wade but once through the "mess," which sometimes makes one question the sanity of the author. But no one who pretends to a general knowledge of the great literary productions of the world, should omit to read the book once.

I might go on to mention many other "famed" books which should be read once by one seeking an even cursory knowledge of standard literature; and whether they will be re-read will depend upon the individual taste or inclination of the reader. One who is not of spiritual bent will not spend much time in dwelling upon the "Confessions of St. Augustine," or Thomas à Kempis' "Imitation of Christ"; and many are even willing to rest their religious aspirations upon a single reading of the Bible, with their memory refreshed by repeated quotations from the pulpit. Great poetry does not appeal to some and they feel that they have paid a sufficient tribute to Milton by once reading "Paradise Lost" and have done their duty to Dante by a serious, if futile, effort to appreciate (in inadequate translation) the grandeur, the beauty, the wit and the knowledge of human nature of the "Divine Comedy."

Finally, I mention one "book of power," "Moby Dick," which would never have been brought to the attention of hundreds of thousands of readers if, *mirabile dictu,* it had not been dramatized and put upon the moving picture screen. That the extraordinary literary quality of this book should have been obscured for nearly a century might have been cited by the elder Disraeli as one of the "Curiosities of Literature." In the style and text of the plot the book is of high quality. Indeed, in the climactic chapters where the hero of the tale approached his fate, the author rises to heights of tragic power hardly excelled in Macbeth and Lear. But the long, interpolated chapters on the history and technicalities of whale fishery (more appropriate in another volume on natural history or the whale-fishing industry), interfere with sustained interest; and the essential facts, much condensed, might well have been woven into the texture of the plot. I have felt that I might some day re-read the book, omitting the technical chapters; and I may then have to revise the above estimate.

Tolstoi's "Anna Karenina" and "War and Peace" cannot be passed over without comment. Both are works of great power. The latter is one of the greatest novels ever written, if, indeed, it can be classed as a novel at all, since in its lengthy digressions concerning war in general and the campaigns of Napoleon in particular, the author made the story the vehicle to enforce his views of International politics and his horror at subjecting the masses to misery and death for causes of which they had no conception. It is a noble, powerful argument. His detestation of Napoleon and his purposes and his low estimate of him as a commander, are skilfully woven into the texture of the plot.

I close this chapter with a saying of Sir John Herschel, the famous astronomer:

Give a man this taste for reading, and you can hardly

fail of making him a happy man. You place him in contact with the best society in every period of history. You make him a denizen of all nations, a contemporary of all ages.

CHAPTER V

CRITICISM

LITERATURE—DRAMA—MUSIC

THE faculty of judgment resides in most men of normal mentality;—and it is more common than the creative faculty. Motives of prejudice, policy or gain may fetter its free expression. But when it is adequately and honestly exercised concerning works of literature, art, and the drama, it may have a vast educational value. Criticism in most ages has fallen far short of accomplishing that result, not because the critical faculty itself has not existed, but because contemporaneous conditions have interfered with its free exercise; and creations of genius have sometimes had to wait centuries for recognition; the works of Shakespeare afford a striking example. Just criticism requires that both the merits and shortcomings of any production should be given their real value in order that a balanced judgment may be arrived at as to its worth. Perhaps all this is commonplace. But it is convenient to state it as the basis for an inquiry as to how far modern criticism has adhered to correct standards.

In order that literary criticism may be adequate, some general, perhaps conventional, method of approach is essential. Some time ago I was asked by the editor of a well-known literary journal to review a then recent book which had caused public comment. My experience had previously been largely confined to reviewing legal publications. To a suggestion that I was deficient in the technique of general literary criticism, the editor responded that there was no such thing as technique; and he imposed no restriction except one as to length—and that I ignored, as the space allotted was inadequate. But absence of plan and scope (in other words technique), tends to make a review a more or less haphazard jumble of comments. The policy of some literary journals is to insert a few extended reviews of what they deem to be important publications and fill the rest of their pages with matter called reviews in which the contents of books are set out with no critical estimate of their style or essential value;—little, where the books are bad, to deter writers and publishers from bringing out worthless books. Literary journals cannot, of course, prevent the publication of such books; and, perhaps, it is too much to expect them to desist from inserting reading matter which will tend to promote their sale.

It is a fact, patent to those familiar with the standard of literary criticism set long ago by the *Edinburgh Review* and the *Quarterly Review* (to mention only two of a considerably larger number), that much of the material in the current literary journals shows inferior ability, is prepared with less care and has a far smaller chance of finding a place in permanent literature, than the reviews of Macaulay, Sidney Smith, Jeffrey, Scott, Hazlitt, Froude, Morley, Symonds and Hayward in England, and of Emerson, Lowell, Holmes and Curtis in America. But the reviews of such writers were not confined to a mere recital of the contents of a book. Often under the guise of criticisms, they contained an independent treatment of the subject matter, expanded so as to become short treatises; and many of them have found a permanent place in literature. But essays, I regret to say, are no longer a favorite form of literary expression; and probably the essay-criticism of the former period would meet scant approval today by the public;—and a substantial measure of popular support is, of course, necessary to the maintenance of a Literary Review. The recent ending of the career of the *Edinburgh Review* after an existence of over a century attests the truth of this statement. The *Quarterly Review* is seeking to maintain the old traditions, and it is to be hoped that it may continue its useful career. Much may be said in commendation of other English Reviews such as the *Contemporaneous Review* and the *Literary Supplement* of the London *Times,* in England, and in America of a very few literary periodicals and the Literary Supplements of some of our metropolitan journals.

Schopenhauer said:

> Under the system that prevails at present, literary journals are carried on by a clique, and secretly perhaps also by booksellers for the good of the trade; and they are often nothing but coalitions of bad heads to prevent the good ones succeeding. Goethe once remarked to me, nowhere is there so much dishonesty as in literature.

But he speaks of conditions long since ended; and, moreover, it is well to guard against the unqualified acceptance of such broad generalizations, especially from the pen of an author who was not devoid of a talent for creating antagonisms. What he describes does not exist today in this country. Between literary departments of magazines and newspapers, on the one hand, and publishers, on the other, there may be friendly feelings, based upon the advertising of new books,* or on quite natural friendship from being engaged in kindred crafts. There may even be discrimination in favor of some destitute but deserving author. These things are not unnatural and probably have some influence; but a more plausible reason for preferential selection for conspicuous notice of a book inferior in merit, is a literary editor's estimate of the popularity and time-liness of the subject and the probability that it will be widely read;—its permanent value being given less consideration. This is the result of the ordinary journalistic motive, to-wit, the printing of what has present news value.

I can in no other way account for the exploitation in reviews of books which, though readable and in-teresting, neither in literary style, nor in the con-tribution to the sum of human knowledge, nor in the qualities of permanence, have a just claim to promi-nence. This is not new in the history of criticism. Something of the same kind prevailed in the time of Hazlitt, who speaks of it thus:

* Note. In an article contributed to the New York *Times'* "Book Review" in June, 1923, by W. B. Maxwell, the English nov-elist, he said: "Books are still reviewed in English papers, because publishers still advertise them. If the publishers ceased altogether to advertise, I do not believe that a book would be ever men-tioned again in the public press."

To elevate and surprise is the great rule for producing a dramatic or critical effect. The more you startle the reader, the more he will be able to startle others with a succession of smart intellectual shocks. The most admired of our Reviews is saturated with this sort of electrical matter, which is regularly played off so as to produce a good deal of astonishment and a strong sensation in the public mind. The intrinsic merits of an author are a question of very subordinate consideration to the keeping up the character of the work and supplying the town with a sufficient number of grave or brilliant topics for the consumption of the next three months!

Schopenhauer would go to the other extreme and make a literary journal a combination of a scourge, a censor and an Academy of Letters. He says:

Literary journals should be a dam against the unconscionable scribbling of the age and the ever-increasing deluge of bad and useless books. Their judgment should be uncorrupted, just and rigorous; and every piece of bad work done by an incapable person; every device by which the empty head tries to come to the assistance of the empty purse, that is to say, about nine-tenths of all existing books, should be mercilessly scourged. Literary journals would then perform their duty, which is to keep down the craving for writing and put a check upon the deception of the public, instead of furthering these evils by a miserable toleration which plays into the hands of author and publisher and robs the reader of his time and his money. . . . Now, most books are bad and ought to have remained unwritten, and consequently, praise should be as rare as is now the case with blame, which is withheld under the influence of personal considerations. . . .

Modern literary editors undoubtedly cast glances more than furtive at the advertising columns and are never forgetful of the predominant public taste; and literary journals or literary departments of newspapers could not today long survive Schopenhauer's ruthless program. Yet there is a tendency even today to regard criticism as unfavorable comment, although that is only a derived and secondary meaning of the word, its original etymological significance being synonymous with "judgment." But the tendency to depreciate is not a mere matter of the correct use of terms. It springs from a quality in many natures to disagree in detail, without giving due weight to the whole. Sir Ian Malcolm cites a similar propensity in those having charge of children to say to one: "Go and see what your brother is doing and tell him not to." It is a truism of journalism that disputes and differences have "news value" not attaching to concord.

A critic having a limited knowledge of the subject treated in a book assigned to him for review, may, after making a recital of the contents, criticize unimportant passages, pick out for comment some slip in grammar or spelling, or dates or names. He thus avoids either a discussion of the substance and prevailing style of the book, but creates the impression that he is standing on a pedestal loftier than that of the author. These critics have been called *Ultra-Crepidarian;* and of them Hazlitt says:

> Littleness is their element, and they give a character of meanness to whatever they touch. They creep, buzz, and fly-blow. It is much easier to crush than to catch these troublesome insects; and when they are in your power your self-respect spares them. The race is almost extinct: —one or two of them are sometimes seen crawling over the pages of the *Quarterly Review!*

What has been said applies particularly, not to the "mine run" of fiction, but to the review of books relating to subjects requiring for adequate criticism a background of special knowledge. Some periodicals and newspapers maintaining Book Review departments are equipped with an adequate reviewing force, or they may assign to other competent persons the review of books for which they are especially equipped. But in many other cases, especially in small towns, reviewers are neither numerous nor well-equipped. The result is often colorless, inadequate and sometimes ignorant reviews; indeed, they are hardly more than news notes of books. A half-dozen books I have published have received, both here and in England, some attention of the reviewers; the trend of the criticisms has been not unfavorable. But denunciation—*concordia discors*—and a resulting controversy, duly advertised, would, perhaps, have had better pecuniary results. I may be permitted to refer to one review of a book I recently published under the title "Kindred Arts: Conversation and Public Speaking." The review was printed in a newspaper of a large town in Indiana and occupied nine printed lines. The writer informed his readers (1) that the author was "scholarly and very proper"; (2) that he was "of the traditions of a by-gone school"; (3) that he was "without a great deal to occupy his time except academic pursuits and the profession of being a gentleman"; and (4) that he was a professor. The review was interesting in its avoidance of any information about the book and for its misinformation about the author. For the author made no pretensions to scholarship. He may have been reasonably "proper" but not "very" much so. He admits a love for old traditions, even if they are of "a by-gone school"; but without knowing what those traditions are, it is difficult to perceive whether the reviewer meant praise or blame. The serious part of the review, however, was that a lawyer, still pursuing his vocation, should be proclaimed as having nothing to do except to be a gentleman by profession, to follow academic pursuits and to be a professor. If his clients, perchance, should see these statements they might (if their case was not so desperate as to require a different kind of a lawyer), overlook his pretensions to being a gentleman; but how would they think he could attend to their affairs if he were a professor and an academician? Finally, the reviewer discovered that the book was *belles-lettres,* as it was intended to be.

I have a real sympathy with the members of the illy paid profession of writing whose thoughts must too often be occupied with the question, whether what they wish to say will or will not appeal to the purchasing public at the next publishing season; and also whether they can speed up their mental processes so as to produce their "stuff" by that time. And my fellow-feeling goes out especially to those who try to make a living as reviewers. The book (above referred to), which I recently reviewed for a literary journal, related to a reform which I had sought to promote in the public interest. There was no other motive for writing the review—certainly not a hope or expectation of, a pecuniary reward. Two days were occupied in reading the book and another in writing the review. Subsequently, the Review sent me a check (returned with the above explanation) for an amount less than one-third of the union wages of a carpenter or a plumber for the time spent! Ought not the benefits of the N R A be extended to reviewers? Probably not, if the incomes of some of the most popular are correctly reported; but if the value of the piece work of the less popular is estimated as I have indicated, how do they eke out a living?

In his charming essay on the "Snares of Criticism," Sir Ian Malcolm lifts the veil and discloses some of the secrets of the craft. To the "lesser daily newspapers" he says he "once contributed criticisms (may Heaven forgive me, for it was my own fault) of about thirty volumes a week."

And he adds:

As regards very many books, there is plenty of internal evidence to show that a large number of reviewers can hardly be believed to have read through the books sent to them; and still more evidence, with regard to more important works, to warrant the assertion that the unfortunate critics had not always the technical knowledge to understand them. It is generally these very people who are in the forefront of the destructive critics;—amateur disciples of Mr. Ruskin, whose denunciation of work that did not please him rang from the housetops, or of Mr. Sneer, who snarled and snapped round every corner.

And he gives a cogent reason for what he describes, since

destructive criticism is an easy occupation; and the nearer the object of his strictures is to the stars the more busily does the little nigger-boy ply his lowly trade.

And then he adds a word as to the kind of criticism we rarely see today:

Sometimes I feel that I should like to have lived in the days when Hazlitt was doing this kind of work, and doing it so well that his criticisms still stand; when Walter Scott and Lord Jeffrey and Macaulay were on the staff of the *Edinburgh Review* and poured out their funds of scholarship in essays upon the greatest new books of their period; when Carlyle was writing in his Chelsea study on Frederick the Great and other famous personages; when John Addington Symonds published his masterpieces on the art of painting; when Mr. Bagehot wrote his biographical studies and the late Lord Salisbury contributed criticisms on foreign politics to the *Saturday Review* in the last half of the nineteenth century. We may, to our advantage, read all of these to-day, if we want classical models of the style and temperament of true criticism.

It is needless to say that we now get few such reviews on either side of the Atlantic; and I repeat that it must be admitted that they would not attract readers in numbers large enough to support a literary periodical, unless lightened in tone by articles of popular interest. It is doubtful whether either

Hazlitt or Macaulay or Montaigne or Emerson or Holmes would find readers eagerly awaiting his next essay-review.

Sir Ian speaks only of the condition of literary criticism in the British Isles. In this country, with the exception of a very few periodicals professing to be literary journals, among the best reviews (I repeat) are those to be found in the Literary Supplements of the Sunday newspapers. But they are not free from the faults and omissions I have referred to. American critics and reviewers are not superior to their confreres on the other side of the Atlantic; and if some of the most popular of them read the books they essay to criticize or recommend, they would have to do so with expedition beyond my capacity and ignore the rules of health as to the time to be allotted for sleeping and eating. But they may have labor-saving devices or even someone to do their reading or thinking; or perhaps they have the gift attributed to Macaulay of grasping the substance of an entire printed page at a single glance.

Despite the fact that destructive criticism is easy, there is much favorable, though undiscriminating, criticism today; and that fact does not tend to improve the quality of the vast book output of this century. The greatness of ancient writers has been shown in that their works have survived destructive criticism.

Homer was charged with stealing from anterior poets; Cicero treated Socrates as a usurer; Plato was accused of envy, lying, avarice, incontinence and impiety; ignorance, ambition and vanity were attributed to Aristotle; Virgil, according to many critics, was destitute of originality, had mediocre ability and was a plagiarist; and derogatory criticism has been heaped upon Cicero by critics too numerous to mention, while Aristophanes disposed of the whole race of contemporaneous poets in four lines:

"Leaves without fruit; trills in the empty air,
And starling chatter, mutilating art!
Give them one chance and that's the end of them,
One weak assault on an unprotected muse." *

An industrious research among the criticisms of the greatest of modern writers would doubtless disclose that few of them have escaped low estimates of their character and abilities. But where the reputations of great authors of the past have for centuries survived destructive criticism, the verdict of time generally prevails over the adverse judgment of occasional detractors, however eminent. Unfortunately,

* Note. Prof. Gilbert Murray's translation of the "Frogs."

unjust contemporaneous criticism may have to await the lapse of generations for its refutation.

We are too apt to assume that the production of a literary work of genius indicates a prevailing culture of which it is the natural expression. Perhaps the assumption has some foundation in the popularity among large groups of the people of the dramatic productions of the Elizabethan period, notably the plays of Shakespeare and Beaumont and Fletcher; and also of the wide appreciation during the Renaissance of the great artistic creations of that period. But at such a distance of time it is not easy to make a comparative estimate of the extent to which appreciation of and taste for the products of literary genius prevailed among the masses of the people. In the drama, however, the culture and the taste of a people may be discovered by the character of the plays they patronize; and it often happens (it is happening today), that their taste is not for the best. In Spain, when he was creating his great work of genius, Cervantes deplored the quality of the drama then popular with the people. What he put in the mouths of the priest and the canon in his great romance is so pertinent to the situation in the present age that I cannot forbear to extend this chapter by inserting much of the colloquy:

The canon first speaks:

I was discouraged . . . whenever I reflected on the present state of the drama and the absurdity and incoherence of most of our modern comedies, whether fictitious or historical: for the actor and author both say, that they must please the people, and not produce compositions which can only be appreciated by half a score men of sense; and that they had rather gain subsistence by the many, than reputation by the few. . . . I have occasionally endeavored to persuade theatrical managers that they would not only gain more credit, but eventually find it more advantageous to produce better dramas; but they will not listen to reason. Conversing one day, with a fellow of this kind, I said, "do you not remember that a few years since, three tragedies were produced which were universally admired; that delighted both the ignorant and the wise, the vulgar as well as the cultivated; and that by those three pieces, the players gained more than by thirty of the best, which have since been represented." "I suppos you mean The Isabella, Phyllis, and Alexandra"; he replied. "The same," said I, "and pray recollect that although they were written in strict conformity to the rules of art, they were successful: the whole blame, therefore, is not to be ascribed to the taste of the vulgar. . . .

"Signor canon," said the priest, "you have touched upon a subject, which has revived in me, an old grudge I have borne against our modern plays, scarcely less than that I feel towards books of chivalry; for, though the drama, according to Cicero, ought to be the mirror of human life, an exemplar of manners, and an image of truth,—those which are now produced, are mirrors of inconsistency, patterns of folly, and images of licentiousness. . . . Thus is

99

our national taste degraded in the opinion of cultivated nations, who, judging by the extravagance and absurdity of our productions, conceive us to be in a state of ignorance and barbarism. It is not a sufficient excuse to say that the object in permitting theatrical exhibitions, being chiefly to provide innocent recreation for the people, it is unnecessary to limit and restrain the dramatic author within strict rules of composition; for I affirm that the same object is, beyond all comparison, more effectually attained by legitimate works. The spectator of a good drama is amused, admonished and improved, by what is diverting, affecting, and moral, in the representation; he is cautioned against deceit, corrected by example, incensed against vice, stimulated to the love of virtue. Such are the effects produced by dramatic excellence, but they are not to be expected on our present stage: although we have many authors, perfectly aware of the prevailing defects, but who justify themselves by saying that in order to make their works saleable, they must write what the theatre will purchase. We have proof of this, even in the happiest genius of our country, who has written an infinite number of dramatic works, with such vivacity and elegance of style, such loftiness of sentiment and richness of elocution, that his fame has spread over the world: nevertheless, in conforming occasionally to the bad taste 'of the present day, his productions are not all equally excellent.

This was written perhaps four hundred years ago. With minor changes in references and illustrations, is it not strangely applicable to conditions of the contemporaneous drama?

Any degradation of the stage today is not due to

lack of ability in the actors,—indeed, they are to be pitied that in many popular plays they are required to debase their talents in the interpretation, both in the theatres and in the movies, of so much that is trifling, coarse and erotic. If in points of composition the plays of today are not inferior to those of forty years ago, yet in the subject treated and in the clever and amusing, but impure, implications of the language employed, there is a lowering of a proper standard of good taste. We may bring forward as examples of the commercial success of meritorious plays, such, for instance, as "Disraeli" and "House of Rothschild," in which Mr. Arliss acted; but we will not persuade the managers to become pioneer reformers and they will continue to proceed on the line of least resistance and rely for popularity upon the drawing qualities of the plot and the lines, even though they verge upon the indelicate. Unfortunately, from the business standpoint we cannot question their judgment; and perhaps we shall not have a reform until there is a reaction from the excesses resulting from lack of restraint. But the policy or the efficacy of a censorship will not avail. A recent effort has been made by the Catholic clergy to improve the character of the cinema plays. It has received the support of other denominations. It has been favorably received by the managers, since it gives them support in reforms which they themselves have wished to make, but which they believe the public would not welcome. Before the voices of actors were synchronized with action shown on the screen, it was seen that something must be done to prevent the vast, growing and popular form of entertainment from having a pernicious influence upon the taste and even the morals of the public.

At a Congress of the Motion Picture Arts held eleven years ago, I made an address in which I stated that the Congress was a

project to save the motion picture industry from possible degradation as a social force, and to make the screen a vehicle for cultivating a taste for the beautiful, the artistic, and the true, instead of suffering it to sink to a point where it may pander to false standards in art and merely beguile the public with episodes in exaggerated, abnormal, thrilling, or frivolous aspects. . . .

. . . The motion picture has an influence for good or evil far greater than that of the legitimate drama or current literature. Potentially, its power exceeds that of the press and even that of the pulpit. The possibility of its being directed into the wrong channel may well disturb us.

. . . Fortunately, the mechanical perfection of the cinema and the commercial stability of the industry have made the movement more than merely chimerical. The time is ripe to achieve the moral, intellectual and artistic uplifting of the millions of people to whom the motion picture now affords chiefly excitement, diversion, and amusement.

*   *   *

But if such conferences as this succeed in making pictures more than mere devices for presenting exciting or amusing episodes, without stimulating thought, or tending to cultural development, or presenting elevated ideals of conduct, there will be erected among us an instrument of immense value for the improvement of our civilization.

Although the Congress was sponsored by the Authors League of America and the leading motion picture producers, extended through two days and was addressed by eminent authors, dramatists and leaders in the industry, no effective steps were taken to put into practical effect its expressed purposes. And since that time with the introduction of the talking feature of moving pictures, their potentiality for good or for evil has been enormously increased. But there has been no material change in the subjects of the plays produced. Many of them are of the type produced on the legitimate stage and reveal numerous phases of the activities of the underworld which have no justification in any moral they purport to inculcate. Thrills, repeatedly produced by various forms of crime, especially in highly colored aspects, can rarely have any elevating influence either on the taste or the morals; while among some of the millions composing the audiences, particularly the young and impressionable, they sometimes arouse through suggestion a dormant spirit of emulation. Furthermore, crime is not always presented in a repellent aspect. Such works as these are met with in literature and on the stage in all ages. But the number of people they have reached in any community has been relatively few; and only plays of rare genius live. On the other hand, the audiences in the moving picture houses of today number many millions, a large proportion of whom are children or adolescents in a formative stage of mental and moral development. Upon the consciousness of these is impressed, without effort on their part, plays of mediocre dramatic quality, tolerated (even by the producers), only because of the sensational subjects dealt with. In plays dealing with marital infelicity and eroticism, the undisguised and alluring realism often displayed is frequently exaggerated, and certainly is not of a character which in real life is displayed in the presence of intruders; and it is often accompanied by postures, gestures and words of *double entente,* having unmistakable implications of indelicacy, sometimes artfully veiled by a humorous setting and witty lines; and the emphasis placed on such realism has recently found expression in profanity of the coarsest type.

Persons of respectability and having a decent regard for the proprieties of life, and particularly women and children, would be inclined to withdraw from any social gathering where oaths derisive of things sacred to them or couched in phrases of indelicacy, are heard. And yet playwrights have recently written plays, and managers have produced them, which are predicated on the assumption that people will pay a large entrance fee to listen to such exhibitions; and unfortunately the assumption is by no means all wrong.

If authors write such plays as I have referred to upon the theory that the American people, young and old, are so sophisticated that they can produce no shock of disapproval and arouse no revulsion of feeling, that would afford an explanation, perhaps even a palliation. But if there is any truth in the assumption, it is a deplorable phase of our social life, and it is to be hoped that it will soon pass away.

What I have said fortunately does not apply without worthy exceptions, either to the stage or to the screen, but that it exists to such an extent as to require correction cannot be gainsaid. Much that is produced in the moving picture theatres is elevating, interesting, inspiring and educational. Their potentiality to exert an elevating influence, and to carry some ideas of culture to millions of people, even those in the most remote hamlets of this great country, imposes upon them a heavy responsibility not to abuse the power thus vested in them by their control of what is said now to be the greatest commercial industry in this country. And there are encouraging signs that they realize that in the faithful and high-minded discharge of that responsibility lies also commercial prosperity. The hope that they can succeed in making an improvement rests in the good sense and moral purpose of the people. But it takes time for an appeal to them to make progress; and especially because objectionable features are intermingled with much that gives harmless and engrossing entertainment, teaches salutary lessons, or imparts useful information.

I turn now to some phases of contemporaneous musical art (I refer to good music, not "jazz"). In that art, both in composition and production, much depends for success on the taste and emotion of laymen, and they form the majority of the people; while on the other hand the principles of composition and the technique of production must depend on the professionals. To bring these together on a basis of mutual sympathy and appreciation is difficult. There are those who believe that the menace to the development of musical art in America is that it is too much under the domination of the narrowing professional spirit and is, as a result, receiving too little of the inspiration and enthusiasm of the amateur. In his book "The Dilemma of American Music," Daniel Gregory Mason has expressed this in the following words:

The lack of breadth, solidarity and pervasiveness in our musical life is not only too apparent to any candid observer, it does not range freely up and down through our whole society, but separates into layers of thin froth at the top, dregs at the bottom, and, to let the metaphor have its way, very little that is either nourishing or refreshing where the beer ought to be. In other words the "highbrows" and the "lowbrows" divide our music between them; the plain man has no use for it and leaves it severely alone, much to his own loss and to that of music. What are the reasons for this neglect, either contemptuous or bashful, of music by the plain man, and what hopeful signs are there that it may be modified?

In the widest most general terms it may be said that in all periods it has been the amateur spirit, the personal love for music and personal effort to participate in making it, with whatever technical limitations, that has brought the plain man and music together; and that, on the other hand, it has been the professional spirit, the regard for high technical finish above aesthetic emotion, the contempt for limitations and imperfections, that have separated them.

107

Referring to the tendency of Americans to rank "science far above art," he continues:

> The life giving amateur spirit has largely succumbed to large scale production under professional expert direction. The dangers of such a course, it is true, have begun to arouse our critics. . . . Movements towards a more free, individual, and joyous creative activity have spontaneously arisen in several fields, notably in the theater. They begin to appear, somewhat uncertainly, in music.

These expressions naturally did not escape dissenting voices. But whether or not they over-stated the situation, they are measurably true of any art where there is excessive specialization. Music requires for its development the sympathetic cooperation of the people, and for the practical reason, both in this country and abroad, that orchestral or operatic productions are rarely self-supporting. Criticism of individual orchestral and operatic productions have for generations been published in the daily newspapers. Only through them can they reach the public, or the "plain man," in Mason's phrase. Through that medium all the noted critics, such as Fincke, Krehbiel, Hale, Huneker and Henderson, to mention but a few, have expressed themselves. What they have said in books or in musical periodicals does not reach the masses and is generally designed for professionals or those who have had a musical education.

In Mr. Henderson's helpful book, "What Is Good Music," he says:

The right to like or dislike a musical composition without giving a reason has long been regarded as co-existent with human freedom.

I imagine that some professional musicians and composers who regard long hair and eccentric attire as essential to virtuosity, and critics who write rhapsodies instead of understandable criticisms, will regard this declaration of independence as crude musical Bolshevism; and yet it is founded on a truth which excessive professionalism is apt to forget, that is, that while composition and the rendering of music to a large extent involves the exercise of the intellectual faculty, the enjoyment of music by the "plain man" is largely emotional. He starts life with an elementary liking for beauty, rhythm and melody as expressed in tunes and airs, and, in more serious compositions, in arias and themes. Modernist composers while adhering to technical rules of composition, seek to produce impressionistic coloring which to the hearer has no ordered arrangement or, indeed, reason, and which, to the ordinary listener, through

109

its dissonances and bizarre devices, sacrifices what to his elemental instincts is beauty,—an important, if not the chief, goal of musical art. Mr. Paderewski has said of modern music that it is "indistinguishable from the fierce hubbub of those mass-production factories to whose recklessly unregulated output the present-day economic confusion is essentially due." The attitude of some of the modernists was summarized in the generalization of one of them that melody was merely a cunning device of music publishers to sell their scores. But whatever merit, artistically and intellectually, there may be in modernistic music and however important it may be to develop progress in the musical art, it is not too much to say that unless the composer pays more attention to the emotional effect of his music on listeners, there is danger that the growth of interest of the public in good music will be retarded.

Why should one who knows nothing of the principles of composition, or the technique of rendering, but who loves the "true concord of well-tuned sounds," not have preferences among classical compositions, and why should he not express them, even if what he enjoys is old and conventional and even hackneyed? And why should not professional musicians take note of such preferences? If the lay listener prefers the Fifth Symphony of Beethoven to the Ninth or any other; and if Schubert's unfinished Symphony and Dvorak's New World Symphony appeal to him; and even if he prefers "Meistersinger" and "Lohengrin" to "Parsifal" and the "Ring," and has a more enjoyable evening listening to Louise and Cavaleria Rusticana than to the operas of any American composer yet developed; and, finally, if he thinks that "Emperor Jones" is wholly unfitted to be put on the operatic stage;—why should he not freely express his preferences and opinions, and why should not his preferences be respectfully weighed by the impresario, whatever a dogmatic and erudite newspaper critic may say in Corinthian rhetoric?

I am writing as one who loves music and during many years have attended concerts and operas, but without previous preparation by examination of scores and with only cursory attention to the libretto. I seek the transitory emotional enjoyment and sometimes the stimulating and elevating influence of the production. I early acquired a taste for good music, not from any musical training but from habit and a fairly correct ear. Perhaps the acquisition of taste for good music in this way is superficial and more or less accidental; but there is little doubt that the popularity of jazz and other productions of that order militate against the support by the common people of a better class of music; and despite some evidences referred to by Mr. Mason that there is a growing interest among the students in colleges for good music, it is a deplorable fact that at symphonic concerts and the opera relatively few young college graduates are seen.

But how do these observations bear on the question of music criticism? Very directly, because there is so much elaborate, apparently very learned, and often rhapsodic newspaper criticism of both the symphony concerts and operatic performances. Perhaps a lover of music who is not trained in the literature and technicalities of the musical art, should hesitate to say that the wealth of foreign nomenclature, technical terms and poetic flights to show the symbolic meaning of portions of a composition, are mere pedantry; for he has not the knowledge which justifies him in making that charge. But it can be said that that kind of criticism will be read understandingly principally by the professionals and a relatively few educated amateurs. It fails to lure, indeed, it tends to repel, the "plain man" who has a taste for good music; and it fails in the high and useful purpose of explaining to him in direct untechnical terms the meaning of what he wishes to know. Such criticisms may be reserved for musical reviews and books, but there they will be read and enjoyed or condemned, as the case may be, only by the elect.

It is not easy for one who enjoys listening to good music to analyze its effect upon his emotions. He knows that music is written to express certain physical conditions and certain emotional states. He can understand that a dirge indicates sadness and solemnity; that dance music is associated with gayety and a corresponding rhythm in the movements of the dancers; and that martial music by a brass band symbolizes war. But music critics, particularly those gifted in rhetorical expression, read into music concepts of the imagination which sometimes remind one of the fanciful shapes that an imaginative person sees in the flames of a wood fire, or in rapidly changing clouds driven across the blue sky in fantastic forms. Mr. Henderson cites an example where a critic saw in the music of Beethoven's Seventh Symphony "spirit shapes . . . now ascending, now descending" who were bashful "as though loath to divulge their secret"; but who finally united "in loving embrace, resuming their song of joy with dithyrambic fervor." And we may agree with Mr. Hen-

113

derson that the rhapsody of the critic was explained
"not in the music but in his own imagination."

Such flights as these occur far more frequently in
criticisms of symphony concerts than of the opera,
whose librettos impose limitations in attributing
imaginary meaning. But I have a weakness for the
esoteric descriptions in concert programs of the numbers to be rendered, not so much that they are of
assistance in understanding the music (for I generally have difficulty in detecting in the music what
the commentator has attempted to prepare me for),
but because of the literary style and the descriptive
power of the writer.

Mr. Henderson, with whom Mr. Mason seems to
be substantially in accord, has expressed some views
which are pertinent in the above observations:

As I said at the beginning of this work, no rule can be
laid down for recognizing the excellence of a musical idea.
Such recognition belongs to the intuitions of the mind. I
am well aware that in saying this I contradict a general
belief that people have to be educated up to a recognition
of excellence in musical ideas. That, however, is only true
of people who have been educated down to something else.
People who have been brought up on dance music,
variety-stage songs, and music-hall ditties have to be educated up to Beethoven and Wagner. So do people who
have never been in the presence of any art at all, musical
or pictorial. But even these people very speedily learn to

perceive the superiority of Beethoven's melodic ideas to those of David Braham.

This was written nearly thirty years ago and despite the hold that good music has upon a limited, and probably a not much increasing number of people, "dance music, variety-stage songs, and music-hall ditties" have lost none of their popularity. A person preferring that kind of music need not be "educated up" to a point where he acquires a pedantic or intellectual taste for higher music and deny himself the diverting enjoyment of light music;—for even in the serious occupations of life we are better for carefree amusement.

But there can be inculcated in the "plain man" in no long period a sufficient knowledge to arouse an emotional interest, and stimulate a discriminating taste, in good music. And the highly cultured music critics of our great metropolitan journals may do much to accomplish that result; and particularly if they are diligent to avoid such criticisms as display only their own erudition, and do not reach that vastly greater number who have a rudimentary love of music and whose taste for it could be easily directed in the right channel. It is that intuitive love of music that sometimes, strangely enough, has stimulated the intellect and stirred the emotions of some

of the great men in literary history. Alfieri, the
greatest Italian poet of his time, said that almost
all his tragedies "were sketched in my (his) mind
either in the act of hearing music, or a few hours
after." Milton and Warburton both found music
necessary for their poetic inspiration, while Leonardo
da Vinci had musicians constantly in waiting while
he was painting Mona Lisa. And it need hardly be
added that it was the emotional—the intuitive—
effect of music, and not an understanding of musical
principles that stirred the imagination of these great
men. They were listeners and they probably listened
without intellectual effort. And this chapter must
close with a putative and homely criticism (again
from Henderson) of the "plain man."

For music was, if you please, not matter to be reasoned
about, but just to be listened to and to be enjoyed. "Who
are these fellows," said the concert-goers, "with their prosy
platitudes about music and her dignity as an art? Do we
go into the concert-room to search for the skeleton under
the beautiful flesh? Nay, let us feast our hearts on the rav-
ishing beauty of naked Sound, and let these anatomists go
fall upon their own scalpels."

CHAPTER VI

OBSERVATIONS ON OLD AGE SUGGESTED BY VIEWS OF CICERO, MONTAIGNE AND SCHOPENHAUER

WHEN one has passed the Biblical limit of three-score years and ten, and yet has "strength" which is not, as the Psalmist gloomily affirms, "labour and sorrow," it is not unnatural that he should reflect upon "that which should accompany old age"; and, if it gives him satisfaction, should follow classical examples in giving expression to his thoughts. And so, having at least the age qualification (or is it not a privilege which age bestows?), I determined to put down a few observations, the result of experience and contemplation. Indeed, being deep in the seventh decade of my age, it seemed to me that I might have had some experiences which even Cicero could not have had, since he was only sixty-two when he wrote his famous "Essay on Old Age." But I was rudely shaken out of this complacent state of mind by the publication of a book entitled "The Youth of Old

Age," written by a cheerful old gentleman of *ninety years* of age, still active in his lifelong and interesting occupation as State Librarian of the State of Iowa. One wonders whether, if the famous Roman had lived twenty-eight years after he had written his homily and had reflected on his lengthened experience, he would not have found occasion to change his assertion that

the most suitable defences of old age are the principles and practice of the virtues, which, if cultivated in every period of life, bring forth wonderful fruits at the close of a long and busy career, not only because they never fail you even at the end of life . . . but also because it is most delightful to have the consciousness of a life well spent and the memory of many deeds worthily performed.

For are there not temptations which confront a vigorous man much older than sixty-two? And while such a youthful old man may continue to hold to the principles of virtue, will his power to practice it and to resist temptation continue unimpaired? Perhaps the question is more astute than helpful; for it is disposed of by the modern researches of scientists, which show that vigor and vitality, physical, mental and moral, are not to be measured by years alone.

But before passing to a serious consideration of these things, I stop to inquire whether I ought to deal with the subject at all. For with Cicero's industry, his philosophical education and habit, his knowledge of contemporaneous, and what even then was ancient, history, his wonderful power of bringing to the aid of his arguments concrete facts, he was enabled, without experience in a period of life which is not in the normal man regarded as Old Age, to produce the greatest philosophical treatise on the subject ever written.

Basing his conclusions mainly on what he observed in those older than himself, he has pictured a contented and useful old man in life and his soul surviving after death, in the enjoyment of the Beatitudes. His optimism is unfaltering and infectious. One who would write on Old Age ought to imbibe the cheerful spirit of the great Roman, even if his essay was written before he had been afflicted by the inevitable decay incident to great age. And one cannot fail to be exalted by the philosophic calm with which the essayist contemplates death and the deep sincerity of his faith that it is but the beginning of a state into which the soul enters for eternity, enjoying an existence wholly spiritual. Though his conception antedated the Christian era, it was in striking accord with the faith and philosophy which was afterwards taught by Christ and his followers. Nothing is more persuasive in Cicero's argument than that with faith in the immortality of the soul, the afflictions of old age become a fleeting condition to be borne with fortitude, patience and resignation. Whatever may be said of his other arguments (which I will comment on later), his eloquent homily on this subject will never in any age lose its force with those who have faith in a future existence. And it stands out in discouraging contrast to the lugubrious expressions of Montaigne, the great French essayist, who said:

> If I would have spoken by knowledge I had spoken sooner; I had written of the time nearer to my studies, when I had more wit and better memory and should sooner have trusted to the vigor of that age than of this would I have made a business of writing. . . . Maturity has its defects as well as green years, and worse, and old age is as unfit for this kind of business as for any other. He who commits his decrepitude to the press plays the fool if he thinks to squeeze anything out thence that does not relish of dreaming, dotage and drivelling; the mind grows costive and thick in growing old.

But it must be remembered that when Montaigne wrote this he was less than sixty years old and, moreover, was afflicted with a number of bodily ailments and died not long after. I think we must attribute his statement to rhetorical exaggeration aimed at discouraging old men of failing powers from exhibiting their infirmities. It was not designed to show that old age generally is an unhappy state, as the gloomy Schopenhauer does when he says:

And passing his fortieth year, any man of the slightest power of mind—any man, that is, who has more than the sorry share of intellect with which Nature has endowed five-sixths of mankind—will hardly fail to show some trace of misanthropy.

*　　　*　　　*

From the standpoint of youth, life seems to stretch away into an endless future; from the standpoint of old age, to go back but a little way into the past; so that, at the beginning, life presents us with a picture in which the objects appear a great way off, as though we had reversed our telescope; while in the end everything seems so close. To see how short life is, a man must have grown old, that is to say, he must have lived long.

These expressions show that views as to the possibility of happiness in old age are divergent; nor can it be said that either of them is wholly wrong. If we are to deal with the matter as it is, we shall find many people in advanced years who, through the limitations placed upon them through their inability to pursue their vocations, to continue their habits or to indulge in their usual diversions, find themselves with no substitute which in their partial

121

disablement they can adopt to relieve the tedium of mere bodily existence. Life becomes a vacuum, and despair, not hope, supervenes.

An honorable man, successful in business and without concern as to financial matters, in the course of time having passed the age of seventy, retires from business. He puts others in control and ceases to direct them. He has no literary or artistic tastes; his interest in public affairs is remote, generally confined to uninformed, and perhaps querulous, criticism. His interest in his fellow man who needs assistance has been manifested in spasmodic contributions. By long habit in making money his sympathetic impulses have been blunted. His newspaper reading is largely the headlines. Occasionally he goes to the play or the movies, perhaps to a baseball game. He has a conventional church connection, but is not articulate about religious views. He attends church once a week and extends occasional hospitality to the minister. He contributes generously to the church. Through disabling, though not serious, ailments, he has been obliged to give up yachting, his favorite sport, as well as hunting, swimming and horseback riding. He stays much at home. His few surviving friends occasionally call upon him; and from time to time, and for brief periods, members of his family (who, of course, have other things to do), divert him with hearts and checkers, or some other equally innocuous and simple game. His mild diversions become irksome and after an hour or two even physically tiresome. And yet he lives on, afflicted by no mortal disease and with the prospect of years of physical existence. He has no available way of entertaining himself and there is no one else who can be found to perform that service for him. Neither through taste nor pursuant to a trend previously acquired, has he devoted his mental powers to the acquisition of knowledge, to the reading of stimulating literature, or to any other occupation requiring reflection or contemplation, or other intellectual activity.

No wonder that such a man (have we not all known him?), would find the hours of his old age a dreary void. The consciousness that it is impossible through any effort of his own to vary the monotony of mere physical existence, must inevitably lead to boredom and ever-increasing mental depression; physical vigor only accentuates his vexation of spirit that his intellectual resources do not contribute to his interest in life; and the accumulation of money to which he has devoted his talents, proves to afford not a touchstone of happiness as he had pictured it during his long life, but a source of unhappiness that it has failed in his old age to give him a Utopian existence.

What can he do to extricate himself from the "Slough" whose name is "Despond"? He may drag through years, perhaps to a state of decreptitude, or retaining his mental faculties, such as they are, he may live, exclaiming with Hamlet:

> *"How weary, stale, flat*
> *and unprofitable*
> *Seem to me all the uses of this world."*

Is such an old age avoidable? Certainly not after superannuation has set in. One cannot compensate for early neglect, by belated attempts to cultivate intellectual tastes or to regenerate an "unlettered small-knowing soul," where there is no aptitude, and an atrophied mind has long since failed to respond to anything except the preoccupations of a life in which there has been no thought of adaptation to the conditions of old age. What Cicero affirms of youth may well be extended to the time when a man is forced or chooses to retire from his vocational activities and to enter the category of old men. He says:

But bear well in mind that in this entire discussion I am praising that old age which has its foundation well laid in youth. Hence it follows as I once said with the approval of all who heard it—that that old age is wretched which needs to defend itself with words (i.e., instead of actions). Nor can wrinkles and grey hair suddenly seize upon influence; but when the preceding part of life has been nobly spent, old age gathers the fruits of influence at last.

I have described above not a wicked or a worthless or an unsuccessful man, or, indeed, one who has not led a life accounted in general estimation as successful; but rather I have attempted to give a true picture of one who has not taken thought to prepare for pursuits tending to produce happiness when old age comes upon him.

The life of man divides itself, roughly, into ages, not Shakespeare's seven, but four, *i.e.,* the periods: (1) of childhood and adolescence, (2) of application, toil and development, (3) of lessening of strenuous labor and enjoyment of earned success, and (4) of retirement and old age. Each of the first three periods should be employed in anticipating and preparing for the next; and in the fourth some thought should be given to the Great Beyond. But I cannot at all agree with the summary of Schopenhauer relating to this subject, however much I admire his strength of intellect and his extraordinary power of literary expression. He says:

125

The cheerfulness and vivacity of youth are partly due to the fact that, when we are ascending the hill of life, death is not visible; it lies down at the bottom of the other side. But once we have crossed the top of the hill, death comes in view—death, which, until then, was known to us only by hearsay. This makes our spirits droop, for at the same time we begin to feel that our vital powers are on the ebb. A grave seriousness now takes the place of that early extravagance of spirit; and the change is noticeable even in the expression of a man's face. As long as we are young, people may tell us what they please! we look upon life as endless and use our time recklessly; but the older we become, the more we practise economy. For towards the close of life, every day we live gives us the same kind of sensation as the criminal experiences at every step on his way to be tried.

*　　*　　*

The main difference between youth and age will always be that youth looks forward to life, and old age to death; and that while the one has a short past and a long future before it, the case is just the opposite with the other. It is quite true that when a man is old, to die is the only thing that awaits him; while if he is young, he may expect to live; and the question arises, Which of the two fates is the more hazardous, and if life is not a matter which, on the whole, it is better to have behind one than before?

What a gloomy, almost shocking, philosophy is this! And, in my view, while it may represent what happens to a few, as a generalization it is a case of inverted subjectivity. At whatever age the author be-

126

lieved that a man would reach "the top of the hill" —whether in a vigorous middle period of life or even in advanced years—his dictum is a gross rhetorical (almost a pathological) exaggeration. Men are naturally sobered as age increases. The "cheerfulness and vivacity" of youth are transmuted, as nature intends that they should be, into the hopefulness of young manhood, and later into the complacence and gratification of middle age,—the fruitage of honorable accomplishment,—and finally into a settled state in old age. As this development progresses, and while most men who are normal will not fail to give some thought to what is to happen to us when earthly existence ends, experience with all kinds of men shows that the general prospect of death does not cause the spirits of men who are in mental and physical health to "droop," or their facial "expression" to change; and it is abnormal pessimism which would hold that it is the "same kind of sensation as the criminal experiences at every step on his way to be tried." I much prefer to accept the philosophy which postulates that death comes to the old as ripeness causes the fruit to fall and that the nearer one approaches death the more he feels like "one who is in sight of land at last and is about to anchor in his home port after a long voyage."

Some men of advanced years—such, for instance, as the one I have described above—may yield to depressing influences. But I speak of the great majority who have arranged their lives in such a way that they have prepared themselves to live contentedly in each of the periods of life as they succeed each other, and adjust their lives to changed conditions as they arise.

And that brings me to consider how a "foundation" can be "well laid" in the early periods of a man's life to give him a fair assurance of a serene and happy life after his retirement from the period of his activity and even into old age. Cicero says:

> Life's race-course is fixed; Nature has only a single path and that path is run but once, and to each stage of existence has been allotted its own appropriate quality; so that the weakness of childhood, the impetuosity of youth, the seriousness of middle life, the maturity of old age—each bears some of nature's fruit, which must be garnered in its own season.

Quite true. But what "appropriate quality" has old age? What fruit has it to garner if the seed has not been sown, and production has not been induced, during the earlier years of life? And what kinds of seed are to be planted? They are as varied as the characters, intellects and physiques of men; and it would not be useful to do more than touch upon the general principles which should govern.

I shall not deal with what may be done to conserve one's physical strength against the increasing weakness due to the weight of years. Nothing is better for this than regularity and moderation in work, diversions and diet. If these produce health and strength, they remove a common source of unhappiness in old age. But bodily vigor will not alone afford a foundation for serenity. Indeed, it may make discontent more poignant because it is not accompanied by a corresponding activity of mental powers or a preoccupation with spiritual speculations; and the numerous phases of such activity and such preoccupation must be looked at to ascertain how far they may be conducive to happiness; and also whether they can be expected to operate unless some approach to them is made in earlier years.

Our minds are always engrossed by their own functioning. We are fascinated when we have an original conception and follow step by step to some conclusion, or make it the starting point for a flight of the imagination. An intimate friend of mine, who was a man of wide culture and unusual social gifts, in his later years and after retirement, spent several hours of a day in the solution of problems of arithmetic. Another, a lawyer of eminence, had a hobby of collecting autographs. He also sought to procure, in addition to the signature, in the same handwriting, something of the characteristics of the writer having historical or other interest. On the basis of the resulting collection (one of the best in existence), he wrote several interesting and instructive books. Even the collection of postage stamps, besides being a diversion, may be so conducted as to be conducive to the study of geography and governmental and social conditions in every country of the world. My father, besides occupying himself with genealogical researches, made a study of the stellar system by means of a telescope installed on the roof of our home; and after a visit to Rome in 1869, occupied himself in deciphering and interpreting the somewhat cryptic Latin inscriptions still visible on the ruins.

One of the most contented men I have known was a physician who retired about twenty-five years before he died at the age of seventy-five. He had a taste for reading,—not current fiction, but books which stimulate thought. He was a dilettante in plant life and by reading acquired a wide theoretical knowledge on the subject. At his summer home he maintained a small flower garden planted under his personal direction, in which, with little expense, he experimented with seeds, humus and soil, and devised untried

130

methods. If sometimes he found difficulty in arousing the interest of his visiting friends in his methods and discoveries, the results always excited their admiration; and he was much beloved by them for his kindliness and unselfish devotion to his hobbies. But his own gratification was not dependent on the commendation of others. It came from his own absorption in the exercise of his mental faculties. With his habit of reading stimulating literature and the study of plant life carried into practical and successful operation, his last years were spent in happiness and contentment.

Numerous other illustrations might be given of elderly men who, after retirement, have contributed to their happiness by mental exercise of some kind. Some have turned in their old age to the writing of memoirs or the study of history and the arts. Others have employed their leisure in the relief of suffering and in the works of charity or philanthropy, thus awakening in them the consciousness that they are doing good for someone other than themselves. In Cicero's view it was the farmers of the Roman State whose lot was the most fortunate, for

the pleasures of agriculture . . . have an account in the bank of Mother Earth who never protests a draft, but always returns the principal with interest added, at a rate

131

sometimes low, but usually at a high per cent. . . . In those days senators (that is *senes* or "elders") lived on farms. . . . It was from the farmhouse that Curius and other old men were summoned to the senate. . . . Well, then, was there cause to pity the old age of these men who delighted in the cultivation of the soil?

But when "superfluous lags the veteran on the stage" how can I commend to him to take up farming in this day, even though he be a Senator? Senators are no longer "grave" or "reverend" or even "potent,"—neither are they so old that they need consider how they may occupy themselves on retirement.* But if there be elder statesmen ready to surrender their togas, will they find happiness in the mental preoccupation needed in the proper management of a farm? Certainly not if, in their forensic deliverances to gain the good will of the farmer, they have truthfully described his hardships. For it is no longer the case, as it was at the time of Roman prosperity, that the farmer

always has his store-room and cellars well filled with oil and wine and provisions; his entire farmhouse has an air of plenty and abounds with pork, goat's meat, lamb, poultry, milk, cheese, and honey.

Despite what aspiring politicians say, the American farmer who lives on his own farm troubles himself

* One of the most recently nominated is in his thirtieth year.

little to produce, in addition to his crops, meat and vegetables or other supplies for his family; but with a Ford car he travels to the nearest town to buy meat and canned goods or to enjoy the movies, while the young men or women, instead of aiding in the cultivation of the crops, are busy preparing for an advanced education, which, if they ever return to the farm, will be of little use to them there; and in many cases (I think a majority) a high school education would be a better preparation for farming, or, indeed, for any occupation they may choose to enter.

And what other kind of a farmer is there? The Gentleman Farmer; and he may spend a happy old age if he lives on his farm and studies the art of agriculture and the raising of stock and acts like a pilot of a ship, who "while others are climbing the masts, or running about the gangways, or working at the pumps . . . sits quietly in the stern and simply holds the tiller." But it is also necessary that the Gentleman Farmer should be able to meet the inevitable deficit in operating expenses.

If there be those in this age, when the fascination and excitement and comforts of urban life are bringing so many to the cities, who, in their advanced age, will be content to lead the ideal life of the farmer, I know nothing that would be more conducive to attain to that state of happiness in old age to which I have referred. But I know few in our time who have chosen to seek that kind of life except from motives of economy.

"The crowning glory of old age is influence." And that may have been so in the time of ancient Rome when age itself commanded respect. Benjamin Franklin, von Hindenburg, Clémenceau, Gladstone, Bismarck, William the First of Germany, the late Emperor of Austria, and Michael Angelo, to mention only a few, commanded, when they were past eighty, fame and respect. But in their advanced age they had not retired but were at the peak of their achievements. And then there is Prince Saionji. At eighty-three he is the last survivor of the Genro, the group of unofficial Elder Statesmen who, although in retirement, have been consulted by the Japanese Emperor in times of national crises.

But Cicero in speaking of "influence" as the "crowning glory" seems to mean the prestige which leads to deference outwardly shown to those who have achieved distinction; "for" says he, "those very things that seem light and trivial, are marks of honor— the morning visit, being sought after, being made way, having people rise at one's approach, being escorted to and from the Forum, being asked for advice—civilities most scrupulously observed among us and in every state in proportion as its morals are good." But in modern times and particularly in a period of popular government in the form of democracies, the "crowning glory" of old age is not the outward marks of esteem shown to notable persons. For in such governments "influence" tends to decrease in its potency when a man who has served his country well becomes a private citizen, but without the power to translate his influence into appointment to office. For truly and notoriously democracies are ungrateful. We see men of distinguished careers retiring in their advanced years and returning to their homes hoping to enjoy the adulation of their fellow citizens or settling in one of our great cities in the vain hope of pecuniary reward commensurate with the fleeting glamour of their public service; and too often they find that the "bubble reputation" is a receding phantom. "More fickle than the restless sea," fame, rising and falling, sometimes presents ironic contrasts. Thus some institutions of learning (particularly those needing factitious patronage, who, as a wit recently observed, advance by *degrees*), more frequently confer academic degrees upon men on their elevation to high office, and before they have proved their worth, than after retirement with a well-earned reputation for duty well performed.

What I have said of service to the state applies to eminence in other fields of endeavor. Even engineers, lawyers, inventors, captains of finance and industry, authors, college presidents and scientists engaged in research, are soon forgotten in the fast-changing turbulence of modern life—excepting those (to mention but a few), who like Edison, have made permanent contributions to the comfort and convenience of hundreds of millions of human beings throughout the world; or Marconi, who took the initiative in opening up communication by means of air-waves; or Pasteur who developed the germ theory of disease.

I am afraid that "influence" will not, in this fast-moving age, save in a few exceptional cases, long continue as a solace or as a stimulus to old men, but rather as a source of disillusionment because men are shown to be so ungrateful and so soon forget. Something more than a passive and receptive state of mind is needed,—something which gives us the consciousness that we are, in our retirement, as in our activity, thinking things out for ourselves, however unimportant the result may be. When a man who has been active all his life (and of such I speak) gives up his lifelong vocation in which his mental faculties have been employed, nothing can make him so conscious that he is old, and nothing so prey upon his spirits, as the abrupt ending of his habit of thinking out the problems of his active life. Men retire after they have worked hard for many years. They declare that they propose to remain idle the rest of their lives, because they have earned a rest. But the shock of the change gradually breaks in upon them. Often it hastens their end; or they become through a surfeit of entertainment or other inconsequential efforts *pour passez le temps,* querulous, morose, impatient and unreasonable. There are many such cases and often they are not the result of age but of mental unemployment. Such a condition may be and ought to be guarded against. But how can it be avoided by one who has confined the exercise of his mind to the problems arising in his business or profession, and has rarely exercised his mental faculties in anything else, floating along as fate decreed, indifferent to the laying up of a store of things on which to exercise his mental faculties? For such persons it would probably be wiser to continue in business and to "die in the harness"; they would thus probably prolong their lives and lead a happier existence.

What can be expected in the life of a retired elderly man if he devotes himself to recreation, amusement, light reading, and social life? Sports requiring physical exercise, such as golf, horseback riding or hunting, are increasingly denied to him. Indoor games can occupy only a small part of his time; and partners or opponents, as, for instance, at bridge, cannot always be found, or, if found, will not continuously adjust their engagements to suit the convenience or pleasure of one whose repeated efforts to have his friends live *his* life instead of *theirs*. They soon become ingenious in pretexts to avoid his importunities. Even the members of a family cannot be depended upon as entertainers. If some games engage his mental faculties, as in bridge or chess, the physical system rebels at an excess of that kind of exercise, particularly where a spirit of contention puts a strain upon the nervous system. A retired man can buy entertainment or amusement at the movies and the theatre and may vary it with a more active employment of the mental faculties at the concert or the opera. But these and other forms of diversion become in course of time stale and ineffective. Social contacts and conversation with interesting and sympathetic companions may be interesting, but they cannot be depended upon as a regular form of diversion;—they too depend on the convenience and inclination of others.

Then there is the reading of light literature, including detective and mystery stories. This is a means of relaxation for some of our greatest men. It enchains the interest without requiring mental effort. Someone has condemned novel-reading as "the last relaxation of the intellectually unemployed." But it does perform a useful service if it relaxes the intellectual faculties. They, as well as the physical and nervous systems, need rest. And the most worthless work of fiction may accomplish that result. Sir Ian Malcolm in his suggestive essay on the "Pursuits of Leisure," truly says:

Novels have their uses, of a minor kind; taken sparingly as an occasional tonic, or as invalid diet for a patient, or immediately before bed time, they are agreeable and harmless;

and Walter Pater makes an even more contemptuous fling at novels when, in "Marius the Epicurean," he says that

For the long shows of the amphitheatre were, so to speak, the novel-reading of that age—a current help provided for sluggish imaginations.

But a man retired from a life work in which, in one way or another, he actively employed his mental faculties, is not seeking relaxation from the drive of active life; for his whole life is in danger of being nothing but relaxation; and he is faced with the danger of atrophy of his mental faculties from disuse. What confronts him is a weariness because he is unable to find a substitute to take the place of the intellectual initiative by which in his business life he had devised and completed useful projects or had made discoveries or inventions. Whether an adequate substitute can be found depends on whether in the active period of his life he has formed intellectual habits and cultivated tastes for pursuits involving some mental effort, which may be resorted to and from which, without dependence upon the fortuitous cooperation of others, he may, with interest and equanimity, employ such mental faculties as he may still possess.

In what I have said I have not referred only to the *intelligentsia,* the "high-brows," or those favored with superior intellectual culture.ᐧ I have meant to include also the far larger number who in their active careers have displayed in the conduct of their professions or business, some kind of mental activity, of whatever quality it may have been. And it will, of course, follow that preparations for a happy old age will be diversified to correspond with the characteristics of individuals in their "infinite variety." But every variety must be governed in a greater or less degree by the same rule, that is, that interest in the life of an elderly retired man can be sustained only if the active, rather than the receptive or passive principle of his mentality, is employed. Schopenhauer's comments on *dilletanti* give an example to illustrate my meaning. He describes *dilletanti* as "those who pursue any branch of art or learning for the love and enjoyment of the thing." He adds:

. . . The dilettante treats his subject as an end, whereas the professional, pure and simple, treats it merely as a means. He alone will be really in earnest about a matter who has a direct interest therein, takes to it because he likes it, and pursues it *con amore.* It is these and not hirelings that have always done the greatest work.

And speaking of the pursuits of old age, he says:

It is a piece of good fortune if the old man retains some of his love of study or of music or of the theatre,—if, in general, he is still somewhat susceptible to the things about him; as is, indeed, the case with some people to a very late age. At that time of life, *what a man has in himself* is of greater advantage to him than ever it was before.

"What a man has in himself" is, as I have pointed out, variable in different individuals and is dependent on education, environment, taste and opportunity. But it makes little difference what it is if it gives satisfaction because it springs from ourselves. The important consideration is whether it quickens our mental processes, or so stirs our emotions that we are impelled to perform acts of mercy or charity or generosity.

Reading books which arouse only passing emotional excitement or amusement, give diversion and relaxation, but they do not stir in the reader independent and active trains of thought. Something more is needed. Permanent interest must be aroused and that happens only when books leave some permanent impression upon which the mind may dwell and reflect. Books of travel, science and history, which not only arouse interest but also add to one's knowledge which becomes stored for future reference, perhaps as a basis for further inquiry; works upon philosophy or the theory of government, to which the mind reacts either in agreement or opposition—it matters not which; biographies and autobiographies, which suggest historic parallels or contrasts or stir the reasoning powers into activity; books portraying the suffering of mankind, cruel or inhuman treatment of human beings, arousing into activity instincts of compassion and justice and inciting us to join in measures of charity or relief;—such books as these, and many others, according to the taste of the reader, will tend to give to his mind and soul something to reason and speculate upon and thus employ his time and attention in such a way as to give him an inner consciousness that, without dependence upon others, he is of some use in the world. Ian Malcolm has said that miscellaneous reading gives us the chance

of teasing the question, the mind of the author, one's own mind, this way and that—until we feel that we have at last arrived at a conclusion about something.

But an elderly man may overdo reading or any other activity, and he must have recreation and some kind of diversion. Opera, concerts, the play, lectures, baseball, will serve,—any kind of frivolity which gives momentary enjoyment or excites pleasant emotions, without effort and without weariness. He should seek pleasurable excitement, keep his enthusiasms alert, cultivate the society of the young, always being studious to detect any evidence of the flagging of their interest, and above all, repress any tendency to believe that age *ipso facto* makes it unsuitable for him to do things which he has done in earlier years and which still interest him. If he does such things he will combat superannuation and postpone dissolution.

143

Some of the things I have mentioned as diversions may readily be made to serve as means for mental stimulation. Thus, the opera, concerts, the play and lectures, may be made the source of intellectual exhilaration, if they are preceded by even cursory study and followed by such critical analysis as the performance naturally evokes; and even without that, their emotional effect may be morally elevating. Such entertainments should rank high among the pursuits of those past middle age, even when they demand of them only slight mental initiative. Even more engaging is participation in the support and management of religious, charitable, philanthropic or educational enterprises; and largely because in them a man is not only occupying his own mind, but is giving vent to his moral impulses, all for the benefit of those less fortunate than himself. What more noble than this, and what can more surely engross the mind or gratify the soul of one whose life is growing to an end!

I have reserved to the close of this chapter the mention of an avocation for men in their leisure hours which may afford both diversion and mental exercise. I refer to writing. Literary efforts of a lawyer are confined to legal briefs, speeches, contributions to legal journals and daily newspapers, and multitudes of reports on professional matters. These are generally directed to giving information, to expressing definite views and making arguments in their support. In such writings some definite conclusion is aimed at. They fairly characterize what a busy lawyer does who also participates as a non-office-holding citizen, in public affairs. With advancing years a lawyer with such a training, or, indeed, any other educated person may, if he elects to try, become fascinated by attempts to write English—good English; —English which shows the possibilities of our really beautiful language;—English which cannot be written without deliberation;—English, which as Quiller-Couch says, has been revised and revised and revised with the author's "darlings" and infelicitous "purple patches" ruthlessly excised. That was the process which even Cicero adopted in writing his essay on Old Age, for in July, 17 B.C., he writes Atticus from Pompeii as follows:

I am sending you the same composition more carefully revised, indeed, the original copy, with plenty of additions between the lines and corrections. Have it copied on large paper and read it privately to your guests; but if you love me, do it when they are in a good temper and have had a good dinner, for I don't want them to vent on me the anger they feel towards you.

Professional or business work can be done better

in ten than in twelve months, if the two of the twelve are devoted to a rational holiday. Few busy men take such an extended holiday, and, if they did, they might find it a bore. That result can be avoided by devoting each morning of the holiday to writing. Whether a publisher would accept the product is of small concern. There should be no time limit for completion imposed by themselves or by any one else —not even by circumstances. There must be plenty of time to revise, to experiment in the selection of the right word, to choose the best among alternative forms of expression, to reconstruct sentences which have stubbornly withstood efforts to make them express thought. No jig-saw puzzle can offer such a fascinating process. It drives out of the mind any thought of publication; and nothing will cramp one's style (to use a phrase used as slang more commonly than in its literal significance), so much as the dread of the unfeeling judgment of a prospective publisher. For those who do write for publication, Sir Ian Malcolm makes this consoling observation:

Do not . . . be unduly depressed if your efforts are rejected, nor unduly elated if they are accepted, by a publisher. For what really matters is not the public exhibition of your inmost self, but the private satisfaction and the serenity of soul that can be secured by years of devo-

146

tion to any branch of art for that art's sake. . . . For in the end, believe me, it is not money or position or public praise that count for most, highly as they are quoted in the markets of the world; but the sense of well-being, derived from the consciousness of a thing well done.

But it may be said that all of this cannot furnish occupation for the great majority who enter the period of retirement, because they cannot adopt pursuits foreign to their lifetime habits; that in a period when mind and will and body begin to weaken, they cannot overcome a possible aversion to any kind of writing not imperatively necessary, and that it is too much to expect an inarticulate man as he advances in years to become suddenly intelligible.

The objections have force. They require qualification and explanation; and they almost compel me to lay down the weapons of disputation and simply plead: Try the experiment and judge by the result.

There flit about in the brains of all of us (whatever our education, our training, our experience, or our intellectual equipment) fugitive thoughts, disconnected ideas, arguments, views and opinions. We express them in conversation or in personal letters, and they may pass into the limbo which is the receptacle for crude, disorderly, profitless, superficial and incorporeal products of man's mind; and thus sink into oblivion. But such thoughts frequently contain in undeveloped form the germs of ideas which are worthy to be built upon; and any one with a modicum of elementary education (even though his spelling is faulty and his syntax odd), can write them down. That is the first step in the experiment. When it is before you, the critical faculty (which everybody possesses, though in varying degrees), begins to operate; and the slight mental effort in directing the pen, followed by reflection suggested by re-examination, either shows the thought to have no merit or suggests a train of thought leading to some interesting conclusion. It is quite wonderful how with no extraordinary concentration, there may be developed (by what the psychologists call suggestion), from one generalization, a page or two of supporting arguments, of deductions, of illustrations, of amplification, and even, according to the writer's bent, of rhetorical flourishes and imaginative flights. And seeking for the right word to express a thought and experimenting with different forms of expression, have all the allurements that one has in attempting to solve a puzzle or play a hand at bridge, or work out some business problem. Anyone who can talk or write a letter can engage in the process; and if he pursues it as a diversion, which requires him at the same time to use some mental initiative, he will find it most engaging, even though what he writes and revises is not published or intended to be, but on completion goes into the wastepaper basket. And for most retired men in advanced years it cannot but have fascination and give them the satisfaction that they are capable of making a mental effort and are not dependent upon or a burden to their families or others. The process involves no responsibility except that resting upon oneself; it requires no superior mentality; it may be resorted to for brief periods and it may appeal to a man's ambition to produce something which he will take pride in reading to his family and his friends. A select few may seek publicity,—a risky expedient, however, for an elderly gentleman seeking serenity in his declining years, for it may excite adverse criticism or contentious debate.

One outliving his contemporaries naturally misses their companionship. He cannot depend upon replacing his departed friends with those newly found. A sense of loneliness follows. It can often be alleviated by seeking some engaging pursuit requiring mental initiative, without neglecting agreeable and sometimes even frivolous diversions; but it can be greatly intensified by yielding to the first despairing impulse to seclude oneself. That leads to supersensitiveness—to a morbid feeling that mere length of years unfits one for the society of a younger generation, or that one is unwelcome in social gatherings. Such a subjective attitude may and should be resisted through the will power. If it gains control, and, even if physical strength continues undiminished, it may lead to an enfeebled mentality and certainly to unhappy isolation—a problem and a burden to friends and family. A man advanced in years need not engage in youthful sports and there are some other things that are obviously inappropriate for him to do,—good taste and surviving aptitude must determine what. But it will contribute to his own happiness, and will secure companionship, if he retains, or perhaps cultivates, a sympathetic attitude toward the lives and pursuits of those younger than himself. To go to excess in subordinating his own taste and judgment to a convention as to what an old man ought to do or not to do, accelerates the pace at which he approaches superannuation and death. Upon this subject Cicero says that

Just as I approve of the young man in whom there is a touch of age, so I approve of the old man in whom there is some of the flavor of youth. He who strives thus to mingle youthfulness and age may grow old in body, but old in spirit he will never be.

I have attempted to throw upon the subject of Old Age some light suggested by modern conditions. But these conditions have not changed the fact that serenity and happiness in old age is dependent upon the will—the determination that mere accumulation of years shall not produce a self-consciousness reacting upon our spirits and making us querulous or morose and sometimes impatient and unreasonable. If such defects of temperament have existed during earlier years, or are incident to disease or decrepitude or hopeless destitution, they may be beyond the reach of improvement; and increase of years will be far from being a boon. But healthy old age ought not to generate such faults if there be some resource having its inspiration from within and giving occupation to the mind or the soul. Such a resource grips a man in his old age more firmly than in the years when the spur of worldly ambition and the striving for material advancement occupied the energies of mind and body; and it will be a specific preventive of the useless and depressing habit of brooding because our years have been prolonged.

Some time ago there was put in my hands by a dear friend a verse said to have been composed by a man past eighty years of age. It has never, so far as I know, been published. It is so sound in its philosophy and so cheerful in spirit, that it is a fitting close for this chapter.

> *"Age is a quality of the mind;*
>> *If you've left your dreams behind,*
>>> *If hope is cold;*
>> *If you no longer look ahead;*
>>> *If your ambition's fires are dead,*
>>>> *Then you are old.*
>> *But if in life you keep the zest,*
>>> *If from life you draw the best;*
>>>> *If love you hold,*
>> *No matter how the years roll by;*
>>> *No matter how the birthdays fly,*
>>>> *You are not old."*